STAND

Also by Cory Booker

United

STAND

Cory
Booker

ST. MARTIN'S PRESS
NEW YORK

First published in the United States by St. Martin's Press, an imprint of St. Martin's Publishing Group

EU Representative: Macmillan Publishers Ireland Ltd, 1st Floor, The Liffey Trust Centre, 117–126 Sheriff Street Upper, Dublin 1, D01 YC43

www.stmartins.com

Designed by Meryl Sussman Levavi

Endpaper credits: (Front flap, top left to bottom right) Me and my brother, Cary, and our dog, Cabbie, at the house where we grew up in Harrington Park, courtesy of the Booker family; Chris Peters, her son Joseph, and Martin, Joseph's helper, at a town hall at Bergen Community College, taken by Cory Booker; "Silent Sentinel Alison Turnbull Hopkins at the White House on New Jersey Day," Women of Protest: Photographs from the Records of the National Woman's Party, Manuscript Division, Library of Congress, Washington, DC, http://hdl.loc.gov/loc.mss/mnwp.160032; John Lewis © Patrick T. Fallon/Los Angeles Times/Contour RA/Getty Images; Elizabeth Lydia Smalls (later Bampfield) (1858–1959) taken by Allen & Rowell, June 1875 © Massachusetts Historical Society; Daniel Anderl, with permission from Esther Salas and Mark Anderl; Kayanna Spooner by Max Spooner, with permission. (Back flap, top left to bottom right) My granddad and grandmom, courtesy of the Booker family; me and Justice Ketanji Brown Jackson (and Frederick Douglass), taken by Cory Booker; Senator Bill Bradley and Senator John McCain © pool/Getty Images; Jennifer Keelan-Chaffins, age eight, climbs the Capitol steps © Jeff Markowitz/Associated Press; Ms. Virginia Jones and family and friends on her birthday, permission from the Jones Family Collection; my mom at the casino!, taken by Cory Booker; Kevin Batts, taken by Cory Booker

The Library of Congress Cataloging-in-Publication Data is available upon request.

ISBN 978-1-250-43673-3 (hardcover)
ISBN 978-1-250-43674-0 (ebook)

First Edition: 2026

10 9 8 7 6 5 4 3 2 1

To my mother

There is no greater blessing in my life
than being your son.

You have always urged me to believe in
impossible things—

to choose faith over fear,

to trust that bold, boundless love is not an end,
but the way to go.

You and Dad used to sign your letters,
"Love eternally."

I never fully understood those words
until he was gone.

Now I know: Death can end a life, but never a love.

Thank you, Mom, for giving me a lifetime of
transcendent love.

I stand because you and Dad so love me.

Contents

Preface

NIGHT HAD FALLEN. SUPERSTORM SANDY HAD crashed ashore and was now headed our way. Meteorologists warned that the hurricane would be an event unlike any seen in our lifetime. I was the mayor of Newark, New Jersey, and decided that I wanted to take one more sweep of the city before hunkering down at our emergency command center.

Two police detectives and I set out in a sturdy SUV that swayed like a golf cart against the gusts of the storm. We encountered few cars. I was relieved. Most had heeded our call to get off the streets and get to safety immediately.

As we traveled down a long stretch of road leading into the city's West Ward, my phone vibrated. I answered.

"Hello, this is the White House operator. Will you hold for the president of the United States?"

A thought that came to me: That had to be the stupidest question in America.

I asked the operator jokingly, "Umm, has anyone actually ever said no to that question?"

No response. Just an uncomfortable pause. I jumped back in with a "Yes, I'll hold."

The next voice I heard was that of President Barack Obama. He was checking in on our city and assured me that no matter the extent of the damage wrought by the coming storm, he would work with us at every step in the recovery. Barack Obama is a man of deep decency; it was a human call more than it was an official one. I hung up feeling grateful.

The call ended, then my phone rang again. It was almost as if the two men had coordinated the timing.

"Cory. . . ." It was Governor Chris Christie. Then the Republican governor of New Jersey, he was also checking in on how we were doing, and again, it was a human call more than an official one. I was grateful for his leadership as we discussed plans for what we knew would be difficult hours and days ahead of us.

In the span of minutes, I had spoken to the most powerful person in our country and the most powerful person in our state. Both men showed professionalism and a focus on their roles and responsibilities to serve in a crisis. Both also extended concern and kindness to me personally. I was grateful for their support of our city and for their compassion. I sat back in my seat as we started up a hill. It was difficult to see through the windshield as it was punished by the driving rain, but I made out a distant light waving back and forth at the top of the hill. As we came closer, I realized that it was a man swinging a light in the street.

Then I saw it: Behind him, large trees had already come down and pulled wires and poles with them. It was a crush of fallen debris.

We slowed to a stop. I could now see the man more clearly through my side window. He was elderly, wearing a yellow rain slicker, and holding a sizable light. I rolled down my window.

Raising my voice over the wind, the rain, and the increasingly powerful storm, I shouted, "Sir! Sir! What are you doing out here?!"

This elderly man—standing in a raincoat, in the dark, in the middle of an unprecedented storm—seemed surprised.

He looked at me as if I had just asked *him* the stupidest question in America.

"Look at this!" he shouted back, pointing to the shattered wood and downed wires. "I'm out here to make sure no one comes along and gets hurt!"

I had just talked to the president of the United States of America.

I had just talked to the governor of the state of New Jersey.

I was the mayor of New Jersey's largest city.

And here was an elderly man, who held no office, standing defiantly in a storm, in the dark of night, risking his safety to hold up a light so his neighbors would not get hurt.

This man, whose name I never got, affirmed perhaps one of the most important lessons of leadership.

Leadership is not a title or position. It is action and example. It is sacrifice and service. It is—especially in a crisis, in the face of uncertainty, in a moral moment—standing up.

Introduction

THIS BOOK IS ABOUT VIRTUE.

I know how that might sound—lofty, abstract, even detached from the crises we face.

Our nation is fractured. In our communities, and even in our families, tribalism drives us not merely to disagree with but to despise one another. Politics has become an obsession with enemies. Demagoguery is ascendant. Authoritarianism threatens our constitutional principles. Corruption is being normalized. Hope feels scarce. What we are against preoccupies our attention, while the deeper question of what we are *for* is left unanswered.

So I can already hear someone objecting: *Dear God, Booker, our country is in crisis and you want to talk about . . . virtue?*

Yes.

Virtue is not a luxury or an end in itself. Virtue—the disciplined practice of our highest ideals—is the strategy through which we as a nation survive and prevail.

It is how we fight. It is how we win. It is how we heal.

The ten virtues I have selected for this book—agency, vulnerability, patriotism, truth, humility, community, creativity, perseverance, grace, and vision—are practices I have wrestled with in my own life. Over the next ten chapters, I explore how these virtues were the keys to success, survival, redemption, and renewal in the lives of individuals and the life of our country, and I argue why each is desperately needed in this moment. From George Washington to Conan O'Brien, from suffragist Alice Paul to disability rights activist Jennifer Keelan-Chaffins, from Abraham Lincoln to John Lewis, I have looked to the stories of leaders from our past and present, along with lessons I have learned the hard way in my own life, for instruction in our time of crisis and challenge.

In this book, I argue that many Americans who came before us, and many among us today, have consistently proven that virtues are practical: They expand our power, deepen our sense of belonging, and equip us to endure and ultimately prevail. Virtue is a strategy that wins elections, moves legislation, and shapes government priorities. But, most importantly, virtue is a strategy that transcends: awakening our sense of common cause, reigniting our shared convictions, and rekindling the belief that our destiny is bound together. In turn, virtue makes the practical work of governing effectively all the more possible.

In the early days of the Civil War, when the survival of the United States of America itself hung in the balance, Reverend Samuel F. Colt,* a Union army chaplain, captured the essence of the conflict in a piercing question: "Are we a Nation? Or, Have we a Government?"[1]

His question was definitional: Who are we? What do we believe in? What do we stand for? What binds us together beyond laws, policies, or our government's delivery of services?

Our founders, imperfect geniuses as they were, sought to create not only a government but a nation rooted in virtue. They studied and drew from Enlightenment philosophers and debated history and human nature. They knew that the government alone could not bind us; only shared values, rooted in the best of humanity could. Those ideals inspired what was written into the Constitution, and the very idea that our Constitution must be amended and our nation improved by future generations who could redeem their shortcomings and address their imperfections through collective struggle and the democratic process. They also knew, and showed us, that virtues are not self-fulfilling or inevitable. They require constant work.

* Importantly, Reverend Colt was born in Paterson, New Jersey. Dear reader, you will have to indulge me for this aside and others, as my Jersey pride runs deep.

And so, again and again, in every era of our history, Americans have made the deliberate and difficult choice to turn toward virtue to meet their greatest challenges and to rise to the call of our country to make ours a more perfect union.

Now it is our time.

We are more than a government. We are a nation, a people bound by shared bedrock virtues. These virtues are not irrelevant relics. They are disciplines of survival and instruments of triumph.

I know many are feeling scared, angry, hurt, and hopeless right now. It is in times such as these that we again face a difficult choice. There is the inevitable temptation to sacrifice virtue for convenience, to exchange our highest ideals for the false promise of expediency. But we can't abandon our virtues now and hope to pick them up later—sacrifice our binding virtues and there may be no later for our nation at all.

I was raised as a child of the civil rights generation. From my parents and grandparents and their friends, I heard stories of heroism—ordinary Americans of all backgrounds who became the foot soldiers of a movement. People who defied impossible odds with courage, sacrifice, and struggle. Amidst their trying time, when people were drenched in hurt and hope was hard to find, they demonstrated great virtue. For them, virtue was a difficult but ultimately rewarding choice. It became an invaluable weapon of resilience, a shield against oppression, and a compass that guided them forward.

My parents quoted something so often in my childhood that it almost lost its meaning for me. Now that I am older, it compels me and imparts a renewed sense of urgency.

It is a refrain familiar to us all: "If you don't stand for something, you will fall for anything."

The virtues within our history are not soft sentiments or moral niceties.

When things get difficult, they keep us upright.

They are a constellation by which to steer through dark times.

In the midst of a storm, our virtues are our defiant, deeply American insistence on standing: for ourselves, for one another, and for the nation we love and share.

1

AGENCY

You are not obligated to complete the work, but neither are you free to abandon it.

—Pirkei Avot 2:16[1]

On a Sunday evening in early March 1965, a man in New Jersey sat on his couch, watching television. ABC was airing the long-anticipated network premiere of *Judgment at Nuremberg*, the first major American film to grapple with the pursuit of justice in the wake of the unspeakable atrocities of the Holocaust.

The movie, three hours long, was a moral reckoning rendered on screen. But partway through, it was interrupted by breaking news. The broadcast cut to footage from earlier that day captured on the Edmund Pettus Bridge in Selma, Alabama, a bridge named for a man who was once a Confederate brigadier general, then a grand dragon of the Ku Klux Klan, and finally a United States senator.[2]

The man on the couch was no longer watching a

dramatization of a historical trial abroad. Now, he was witnessing a moral trial unfolding in his own country.

That afternoon, around six hundred peaceful protesters had begun a march from Selma to Montgomery to demand the right to vote for all citizens, regardless of race. They were met by a wall of Alabama state troopers. Some marchers decided to kneel and pray, but before they could, the troopers charged.[3]

Batons rained down. Tear gas filled the air. Officers mounted on horseback descended on the crowd. Screams rang out as marchers were clubbed, trampled, and chased. Among them was twenty-five-year-old John Lewis, who was struck in the head and nearly killed.

The scene, broadcast into millions of homes, felt like a tear in the fabric of the nation. As journalists Gene Roberts and Hank Klibanoff later wrote in their Pulitzer Prize–winning book, *The Race Beat*, about the trial in *Judgment at Nuremberg* and the live brutality in Selma, "The juxtaposition struck like psychological lightning in American homes."[4]

The day would become known as Bloody Sunday.

Support for the civil rights movement exploded overnight. By the next day, clergy, students, and citizens were organizing in cities across the country. So many people flew to Alabama to join the protest that the Montgomery airport ran out of rental cars. Many people said the same thing: They had been home watching *Judgment at Nuremberg* when the news broke.[5]

Just over a week later, President Lyndon B. Johnson declared, "At times, history and fate meet at a single time in a single place to shape a turning point in man's unending search for freedom. So it was at Lexington and Concord. So it was a century ago at Appomattox. So it was last week in Selma, Alabama."[6]

But the violence that shocked the nation stemmed from a quieter, earlier injustice: the death of a twenty-six-year-old deacon named Jimmie Lee Jackson.

Jimmie Lee lived with his family in Marion, Alabama. He worked long days chopping wood and, in his spare time, became involved in the civil rights movement. He had repeatedly tried and been blocked from registering to vote.[7] One evening, he and his family joined a peaceful march outside the jail where a voting rights activist was being held. State troopers began attacking the marchers. Jimmie Lee rushed to protect his mother and was shot twice in the stomach.[8]

The closest hospital refused to treat him, so he was taken on a longer drive to the Good Samaritan Hospital in Selma, the only hospital in a six-county area that treated Black people.[9] He died there eight days later.

There were no national headlines. No presidential remarks. But for civil rights leaders, his death was a clarion call. As Martin Luther King Jr. declared at Jimmie Lee's funeral, "You died that all of us could vote, and we are going to vote." He called him "a martyred hero of a holy crusade for freedom and human dignity."[10]

And so, four days after Jimmie's funeral at Brown Chapel, six hundred people gathered, prayed, and set out across the Edmund Pettus Bridge.

* * *

As THE *Judgment at Nuremberg* broadcast resumed, the man in New Jersey, a white lawyer named Arthur Lesemann, sat in front of his TV stunned. His first inclination was to go to Alabama to help, but he had just started his own law practice and couldn't afford to close his office. For a moment, he slumped back onto his couch, feeling despair and frustration about the state of the world and his inability to do anything about it. But then he decided he would not allow his inability to do everything undermine his ability to do something.[11] He would make a stand with what he had, where he was—he decided that he could afford to give roughly one hour more a week to pro bono work dedicated to civil rights.

That led him to the Fair Housing Council of Northern New Jersey, run by a Black woman named Lee Porter. Her organization was fighting discriminatory housing practices and badly needed legal support. Arthur offered his services.[12]

At the time, the practice of real estate "steering" was rampant across the country. Black families were shown homes only in Black neighborhoods, and if they asked about a house in a white neighborhood, they were often told the house was already sold—even if it wasn't.

Arthur and Lee devised a plan. They launched sting operations: Black couples would inquire about a home in white communities. If they were turned away, the Fair Housing Council would send in white volunteers to serve as "test couples." Time and again, the white couples were told the homes were still available. Time and again, Arthur and Lee exposed the lies. Slowly, Black families began integrating towns across northern New Jersey.

Four years later, a case landed on Arthur's desk. A young Black couple had been repeatedly told that homes in white neighborhoods they visited in the suburbs of northern New Jersey were no longer available. The Fair Housing Council set up one of its sting operations. The Black couple visited a house that they loved in Harrington Park, a beautiful small town nestled in the affluent suburbs of New Jersey along the New York border. They were told it was no longer for sale. So the Fair Housing Council sent in a white volunteer couple, who were told that the house was still for sale. The white couple made an offer on the house. Their offer was accepted. Contracts were drawn. A closing was set.

But on the day of the closing, it wasn't the white couple who walked into the real estate agent's office. It was the Black man and a volunteer attorney named Marty Friedman. The agent recognized the Black man and realized he'd been caught.

Marty spoke sharply to the agent, telling him that his actions were illegal. Before he could finish, the agent stood up, cocked his arm, and punched Marty in the face. Then the agent sicced his Doberman Pinscher on the two men. A window shattered. Furniture toppled. The men got out—undeterred.[13]

The Fair Housing Council threatened legal action. The owners, unaware of the agent's behavior and appalled by what had happened, intervened and sold the house directly to the Black couple.

The family moved in with their two young sons—a two-year-old and a newborn. The boys thrived in the neighborhood and the local schools. Their mother went on to become board chair of the Fair Housing Council. And forty-four years later, people in that community and in communities across New Jersey elected the younger son to the United States Senate.

I am that son. This is my story. It is also our story. It is not a story about what presidents, governors, or generals did but about what ordinary people did—people who refused to let their limitations, or the sometimes overwhelming nature of injustice, define their actions. They stood for us. They struggled for us.

Some risked or even gave their lives for us. And some, like Arthur Lesemann, stood up and gave an hour more a week.

* * *

I FIRST SPOKE with Arthur in 2015; by then, he was a retired judge, still living in New Jersey. I was working on my first book and had been trying to trace the story of how my parents came to live in Harrington Park, and I'd spoken to many people, including Lee Porter. Lee had praised Arthur's work and urged me to talk with him directly.

I called and introduced myself. "Senator, I know who you are," he said, without hesitation.

I asked if he knew what he had done for my family.

"Yes," he said, humbly.

I tried to put into words the gratitude I felt—the way his actions had changed my family's trajectory, how much I owed him. My parents had often reminded me that I stood on the shoulders of so many people who had fought battles I would never fully know. And now I was speaking to one of them.

He deflected the praise. He spoke instead of the broader coalition, like the foot soldiers who had made the Fair Housing Council's work possible. And then he spoke of Selma, of the Sunday evening in 1965 when he watched *Judgment at Nuremberg*, and he recalled how the film had been interrupted by footage from the Edmund Pettus Bridge.

It was a turning point, he told me. "What I saw that day . . . it changed me. I knew then that I had to do something."

We talked about the sting operation, about my parents, and about John Lewis, who had become my colleague and friend in Congress. Arthur admired him deeply for his courage, his creativity, and the unwavering moral force of his work. I later had the honor of telling John about Arthur's story—how it was John's stand in Selma that had inspired Arthur to help my parents find a home, which had ultimately changed my life.

What stayed with me the most about my conversation with Arthur was how he talked about the 1960s. The upheaval. The violence. The assassinations. The bombings. The bloodshed. But also, the moral clarity that emerged amidst that chaos.

It was wrong, I remember him telling me. *And it had to change. And I had to do my part.*

Then he said something powerful: *Senator, in times like that, we all have to do more—even just a little more. That little more makes a lot more of a difference than people think.*

I asked him why he thought some people forget that.

He paused. *I don't know,* he said. *But I do know this: There are more good people than we realize. A lot of folks quietly doing good. We are each other's hope.*

* * *

THE HOPE that Arthur talked to me about is a choice. A choice to act, to use our agency rather than abandon it. It's what we do for one another, how we choose to show up.

Hope is the active conviction that despair will not have the last word. Hope is stepping forward even when success seems uncertain. Hope is believing that no act, no deed, no just offering is ever wasted. Yes, hope gets knocked down, hope gets dashed. Hope carries scars and wounds. But still, despite it all, hope acts and never gives up.

Jimmie Lee Jackson was an agent of hope. His courage cost him his life. His loss sparked a movement.

John Lewis and those marchers were agents of hope. Though beaten and bloodied, they rose and marched again, and their courage moved a nation—and a Congress—to act.[14]

Arthur Lesemann and a small community of activists were agents of hope—in the face of injustice after injustice, their efforts changed and shaped the course of my life. Everything I do is a part of their legacy of action.

This is the superpower we all possess: to step forward

even when others shrink back. To do what we can, even if it seems small. Because even the smallest act can echo across time.

Demagogues, authoritarians, and would-be despots want us to forget this. They want us to believe we are powerless. That only they can protect us. That we must trade our agency for their assurances. But the real threat to justice is not in their lies. It's in surrendering to the belief that we don't matter, that our voice is too small, that our efforts are futile.

What an insult to our ancestors that would be.

American history is a testament to the achievement of impossible things against impossible odds by people who never gave up. Our rights and freedoms were not granted. They were won. And those victories most often came from the people *not* recorded in our history books.

We didn't win voting rights because Strom Thurmond stood up on the Senate floor one day and declared, *I've seen the light, let those Negro people vote!* No. We didn't win women's suffrage because one day on the Senate floor, a bunch of guys circled up and said, *Fellas, put it in, on the count of three, let's give women the right to vote, ready . . . 1, 2, 3, SUFFRAGE!*

Again and again, our shared story shows us that great change doesn't come *from* Washington, it comes *to* Washington from Americans who realize their agency and take small but definitive, determined actions against the wrongs they see. Voting rights came *to* Congress. Brought there by people who marched, protested, organized, and sacrificed. People who were beaten. People who were overwhelmed, exhausted, insulted, and attacked. People who, despite it all, acted again and again. Sometimes they lost. Yet, even in devastating defeat, they still sowed the seeds of victory.

Today, the enormity of what is wrong in the world and with our country can feel paralyzing. When watching TV, scrolling our phones, or reading the news, we can feel angry, hurt, and scared, all compounded by the feeling that we can do little or nothing about it.

We aren't feeling overwhelmed by accident. Our cynicism is someone's strategy. There are those who are working every day to make us feel like we are powerless and that our efforts don't matter. This becomes a self-fulfilling state: We get stuck, we agonize but we don't organize, we get outraged but we don't get out working. We surrender to the notion that any action we take will be too small to make a difference.

But that is plainly a lie.

Any fair reading of history, any close examination of our own lives, tells us a different story.

The truth is, we are all more powerful than we realize, more capable than we know, and we all have the ability to make a difference beyond what we can immediately see.

A twenty-six-year-old man in Marion, Alabama, fought peacefully for the right to vote. He was murdered because of it.

His death led some six hundred people to cross a bridge and demand democracy for all. They were beaten back.

Their courage inspired a man in New Jersey, who volunteered an hour more of his time every week. That hour helped move my family and others into homes and changed the course of my life. I, like you, owe my existence to the actions of generations of Americans—most never mentioned in history books, their deeds not recorded, but their millions of acts of courage, defiance, and love changed our world and advanced the nation we live in.

Now is not the time for us to sit on the couch, watching others struggle. Our democracy is not a spectator sport. It demands participation.

Now is our time to stand. To act, even if our steps are small. Even if our time is short. Even if our offering seems modest. Now is our time to remember that we are each other's hope. To remember that we each have agency. To remember that we are powerful.

2

VULNERABILITY

The world breaks everyone and afterward many are strong at the broken places.

—Ernest Hemingway, *A Farewell to Arms*

In the middle of a crowded movie theater, my life came full circle. My mom leaned over and whispered, "You need to take your dad to the bathroom." Just like that, our roles reversed. My dad, my first hero, was now in need of the same help he once so lovingly gave me as a child: a bathroom escort.

My father had Parkinson's disease. I will never forget the moment, years earlier, when I knew the disease would win, despite my father's immense will and grit. We were driving on the highway when he pulled over abruptly. His hands trembled on the steering wheel. He looked at me with an expression I had never seen before, a combination of pain, brokenness, fear, and defeat.

"Son," he said slowly and quietly, "you're going to have to drive."

I nodded and smiled, trying to mask my own fear and anguish. But I knew my father, who was always emotionally attuned, saw through it. That made it worse for both of us. We switched seats in silence. When he slid into the passenger side, he didn't speak. No wry joke to lighten the moment. No effort to deflect. Just silence, and in that silence, a heartbreaking realization. He had surrendered the wheel. And with it, he had surrendered control, independence, and another piece of his pride.

As the disease progressed, so did the toll on my mom—his wife of over four decades. Her love never wavered, but the weight she carried grew heavier by the day. She began doing more and more for him: helping him out of bed, dressing him, assisting him in and out of the shower or bathtub. She threw out her back lifting him and sprained her knee slipping on the bathroom floor. Pretty soon she was not just nursing him but having to tend to her own injuries. And as his Parkinson's-related dementia worsened, the danger deepened.

He began to wander. Once, at a restaurant, he got up to use the bathroom and disappeared. Hours later, we found him lost in the adjacent mall. Another time, he left the house in the middle of the night and wandered the neighborhood. My mom searched frantically up and down the block, calling his name, until a neighbor phoned to say they had found him.

The worst came when he started having moments in

which he no longer recognized her. Once, she was helping him in the bedroom when panic overtook him. He lashed out in fear of this stranger, knocked her hard to the ground, and tried to flee. My mom was badly shaken, but she didn't give up.

My brother and I helped my mom hire caregivers. But even with support, the emotional, physical, and financial strain never let up. My mom fiercely loved my dad through every stage of his decline. But I could see the toll it was taking: the exhaustion in her body, the weight in her spirit, the quiet heartbreak of watching the man she had built a life with slowly fade away.

So when she whispered to me in that movie theater, "Take him to the bathroom," I didn't hesitate. I reached for his hand and called him by the nickname he loved: "Daddy-O, let's go to the bathroom."

As he slowly shuffled down the aisle and out of the theater, my dad seemed to be moving on autopilot. I directed him forward as his shaking arms held on to me. I made assuring small talk as I coaxed him through the lobby, but he didn't respond. I am not sure he could have at that moment. He was absent, his eyes glazed over and vacant.

In the restroom, I guided him to the urinal. I assumed that would be it—he'd relieve himself, I'd help him wash up, I'd escort him back, and we'd have only missed a bit of the movie. But I saw his shaking hands struggle vainly toward his belt and realized that he required more help.

Then, realizing the logistics of what I had to do, my own discomfort started fighting with my full focus on my father.

I was the mayor of Newark at the time. I sometimes got recognized. And as I stood there beside a urinal, in a public movie theater bathroom, fumbling with my father's belt, I found myself silently praying, *Please, God, don't let anyone walk in right now.*

God heard my prayer. Which of course meant that someone immediately walked in.

The person walked past us and then stopped. I was focused on my dad, but I could feel their stare. *Please, just keep walking*, I thought, as this man continued to watch us for what felt like an excruciatingly long time. I was standing at a urinal with my ailing father, struggling to undo his pants and help him go to the bathroom; I felt embarrassed, vulnerable, and worried about what this man was thinking and even what he might do. Finally, with a burst of energy, he spoke: "Cory Booker! Is that you?"

I looked up.

"Oh man, I love you, you are great!" he exclaimed.

I was half flattered and fully mortified. As he continued to share generous praise, I looked at my father, and, incredibly, the absent, glazed look was gone. My dad was fully there; I saw him in his eyes again. And not only was he present, he was thrilled. He completely grasped the situation, saw my utter embarrassment, and was loving every second of it.

The man in the bathroom thrust his hand toward mine, insisting on a urinal-adjacent handshake. I deflected, nervously raising my hands, as if surrendering to a stickup man. As I stammered back at the stranger's generous words, I was incapable of hiding my embarrassment, and my father was incapable of hiding his joy.

At that moment, one of the last times I saw my dad fully present, he was once again the father and I the child. He was the teacher and I the student who, struggling to be seen as cool, was fully humbled. That moment reminds me of how beautiful life can be—not despite the anguish, pain, mess, and difficulties but because of them; because of the fullness of life's experience; because of all of the things we share that make us truly human.

I never would have imagined that walking my dad into that bathroom that day would end up being one of my favorite memories with him, and perhaps one of the most important ones. Now, years after his death, I smile as I think about the smug look on his face as his "big shot" mayor son was brought to ground, squirming and awash in awkwardness.

In the depths of my father's God-awful disease, I discovered more of my own humanity and that of others. Whenever I shared stories about what my family was going through, and when others, in turn, would share their own stories of struggle with aging parents, a partner with a terrible illness, or their own experience with dementia or another degenerative disease, any delusion of "otherness" fell away.

* * *

LONG BEFORE that day, my dad taught my brother and me to be vulnerable. He wanted us to understand that being open about our struggles and trials created the possibility for deeper connection and greater community. And that healing, hope, and redemption could come from that openness.

My father earned that understanding the hard way. He grew up in the segregated South, in stark poverty, born to a single mother who couldn't care for him. His grandmother took him in, but soon she couldn't take care of him either.

Growing up, I knew that he carried scars and trauma from past feelings of abandonment. He would grow visibly uncomfortable and emotional if he heard about a child without parents. Even fictional parentless characters troubled him. I remember he once got up and walked out of a movie theater during *A.I. Artificial Intelligence*, a Spielberg film about a robot boy who was abandoned and unwanted.

My father was eventually taken in by an incredibly loving family that gave him a home and helped raise him and equip him for the difficult racial realities of 1950s

America. By the time he left that tight-knit North Carolina mountain town for North Carolina Central University, a historically Black university in Durham, he had a keen understanding of poverty, discrimination, humiliation, and what it meant to be looked down on, demeaned, underestimated, and even discarded.

He never wore his trauma like a badge. He didn't romanticize his struggles. But he believed that his brokenness gave him more points of connection with others. And that his pain deepened his empathy. The experiences that scarred him also taught him how to listen, how to go deeper than surface conversations, how to find common humanity with others.

My father, who faced early feelings of loneliness and abandonment, came to realize that it is through vulnerability that we discover the truth: We all belong.

He taught me that opening yourself up and talking of your pain and hurt isn't weakness, it is an act of liberation. He loved artists who laid bare their pain, from Billie Holiday's song "Strange Fruit," about the agony of lynching, to the achingly powerful poetry of Langston Hughes, who asked, "What happens to a dream deferred?" I will never forget watching my dad put on a Richard Pryor record after a long day at work in predominantly white corporate America. I watched him react to Pryor's truthful testimony about the absurdity and indignities of racism. I saw it speak to him, see him, and replenish him through laughter. Artists like Pryor took the racism that was supposed to humiliate them and alchemized it into something that helped heal and even activate more people to the cause of defeating it. Many great artists unflinchingly and unapologetically expose their pain to broader audiences and command their acknowledgment and their alliance in addressing it.

My childhood stands in stark contrast to my father's. Two parents. A suburban New Jersey home. I was safe, secure, and privileged. And so my dad, with both love and mischief, made it his mission to humble me, lest I become too proud. He was a relentless practical joker, gleefully embarrassing me in front of friends, always going to great lengths and taking great pleasure in flustering me. The more success I enjoyed and the more public praise I received on the football field, in school, and in public office, the more he enjoyed bringing me back to earth.

Watching their child graduate from Yale Law School might be a time for many parents to feel pride and joy, and, yes, my father felt that, but he also saw it as exactly the right moment to drive home his larger lessons. He looked at me and said, "Boy, you got more degrees than the month of July, but you ain't hot. Life ain't about the degrees you get. It's about the service you give."

My father's lessons to me were about a particular balance: Strive for distinction, yes, but don't set yourself apart. Don't fool yourself into believing that you are better than others or that you don't need people. We all need each other, more than we know.

I think he understood that for my well-being as well as that of all others, service is vital. Service is not about charity, it is about stepping into our shared humanity. It is about discovering our common struggles, our common urgencies, and how truly interconnected we all are. We discover this not when we wear our masks or armor, not when we separate ourselves. We discover it when we open up, when we have the courage to show our true selves, scars and all. When we have the courage to be vulnerable.

The power of vulnerability—the import of sharing one's wounds and worries, one's fears and faults—is that it shrinks the distance between us and reminds us that we are bound together, that we are invested in each other, and that we belong to one another. From that comes greater community, and from community comes an even greater strength. Community affirms, grounds, even heals us. It empowers us to deal with the larger struggles and ugliness of the world.

My father gave me a master class in leadership that I am more and more determined to follow. He believed that his task, our task, was to share heart and struggle, spirit and joy, to show up for those facing difficulties and others in large ways and even tiny ones, like with a smile, kind word, or small gesture. I strive to live up to his example every day.

In my once narrow and limited understanding about the all-too-common experience of disease and dementia, he expanded me—my heart and my community.

My father was my first hero because to me as a child, he seemed like superman. My dad is now my greatest hero because he wasn't superman. He was a man. Deeply human. Even in his final stretch, a boy who had felt abandoned in the world was an incredible man—vulnerable, ailing, yet still teaching.

If you are silent about your pain, they'll kill you and say you enjoyed it.

—author unknown*

IT WAS around one AM on April 1, 2025. I had been speaking on the Senate floor for a few hours, my feet were numb, and I was struggling to hold it together.

For months, people in New Jersey and from all across America had been rightfully demanding more of me

* I've quoted this for years thinking it was Zora Neale Hurston, but my dutiful fact-checker—thank you, Ben—informed me that if these were in fact her words, the work has been lost. Alice Walker has a similar quote in her 1992 novel, *Possessing the Secret of Joy*: "If you lie to yourself about your own pain, you will be killed by those who will claim you enjoyed it."

and other members of Congress. So many of the phone calls, letters, and messages my office received during the first weeks of the second Trump administration had come from people concerned by the changes that Donald Trump and Elon Musk were making or intending to make to bedrock programs like Medicaid, Medicare, and Social Security. Many were not simply upset about the cuts in service and threats to these programs—they were terrified. My staff who answer the phones and open the mail were shaken by what they were reading and hearing.

Just over two months in, the Trump administration and its allies in Congress were threatening to make the largest cut to Medicaid in the history of the program—they eventually did. Musk and his Department of Government Efficiency had gained access to the records and payment systems that administer the Medicare and Medicaid programs upon which nearly a third of Americans rely.[1] And they had already announced a plan to lay off thousands of employees in the Social Security Administration. They said they would be eliminating service by phone, requiring seniors to visit Social Security offices in person to enroll in or make changes to their benefits; at the same time, they announced they would be shutting down many of those offices.[2] The commerce secretary, Howard Lutnick, a billionaire who will never need to rely on Social Security for his basic needs, suggested that only a "fraudster" would complain about missing their monthly Social Security checks.[3]

It's difficult to overstate what cuts to these programs would mean for millions of people—seniors who depend on Medicaid for long-term care, people with disabilities who rely on Medicaid for the services that allow them to stay in their homes and communities and live with independence and dignity, the rural and safety-net hospitals that depend on Medicaid to keep their doors open, or the 73 million Americans who receive Social Security benefits and the millions more planning on those benefits being there for them in retirement. In New Jersey, around 40 percent of the approximately 1.6 million residents who rely on Social Security have no other source of income.[4]

People from all over the political spectrum were stepping up. Some were resigning their posts in government in protest, others in the public were speaking out, many were demonstrating, and seemingly all were rightfully demanding that Congress do more and fight back.

Everywhere I went, I heard that demand. People stepped to me to make their opinions known. It seemed that the more people knew me, the more demanding they were. In Newark, I caught the worst of it, or was it the best? In a supermarket I had convinced to come to Newark when I was mayor, a man caught me in the frozen foods aisle.* He began to give me instructions about what Democrats should be doing in Congress, and I proceeded to tell him all the things we couldn't do because we were in the minority—Republicans controlled both houses of Congress and the White House. This didn't satisfy him. He went in on me.** He told me he had voted for me since I ran for city council in 1998 and that he remembered when I went on a ten-day hunger strike to protest the conditions at Garden Spires, a dangerous housing complex. He said he remembered when I moved into a mobile home and parked it on dangerous drug corners in the city to help those neighborhoods. He said he remembered when I challenged the city's machine politics when no one believed I could win—and eventually we did. And then he asked me, *Where is that guy? Why isn't he showing up now?*

I went back to Washington and knew it was time to show up differently. My team and I had brainstorming sessions. What could we do that wasn't business as usual, that could elevate the voices, too often unheard, of the Americans most directly affected by the decisions being

* It was chilling—sorry.

** A biting rhetorical question from the conversation I still think about often was, "Cory Booker, are you an Ameri-can or an Ameri-cant?"

made? We decided that I would take control of the floor for as long as I could. According to the Senate rules, I wouldn't technically be filibustering—I would, however, speak continuously, without yielding, for as long as I was physically able.

My team and I discussed trying to break Senator Strom Thurmond's record in the process. It had always bothered me that Thurmond—a man who at one time would not have wanted to share a bathroom with me, let alone the title "senator"—was remembered and in some ways revered for holding the record for the longest speech in the world's greatest deliberative body. In 1957, Thurmond had spoken on the floor for twenty-four hours and eighteen minutes, attempting to block the Civil Rights Act of 1957.[5] He succeeded in setting the record for the longest speech on the Senate floor, but he failed to stop the Civil Rights Act from advancing.

But even if I didn't beat his record, I thought we could still at least do something that would make a mark, that would break through, at a time when people were demanding that their representatives in Washington do *something*. So we started putting together material. If I was going to hold the floor, I didn't want to read *Green Eggs and Ham*—I wanted to present a coherent, substantive accounting of the crisis facing our country.[6] We brainstormed and wrote about different topics, from threats to Social Security and Medicaid to the rule of law and national security. We collected articles, reports, and stories and sifted through letters from New Jerseyans and others who reached out. We wanted to center their voices in my speech. And we came up with a plan: My team was going to split up over 1,164 pages of prepared material into more than a dozen binders that I would read from throughout the night and the following day. And I prepared my own binder—full of some of my favorite poems, stories, and quotes from history that over the years have inspired and sustained me. I knew they would give me strength during the challenge ahead. It included Emma Lazarus's "New Colossus," which is inscribed on a plaque at the base of the Statue of Liberty, and Langston Hughes's "Let America Be America Again."

And then there were more practical considerations. According to the rules of the Senate, holding the floor meant that I could not sit down and that I certainly could not leave to go to the bathroom. Some actually suggested wearing a diaper—I believe in courageous vulnerability, but peeing my pants on C-SPAN is a step too far. So I concluded that dehydrating myself was my only option. Three days before, I stopped eating. More than twenty-four hours before, I stopped drinking water. In between, knowing I wouldn't be able to drink coffee,

I experimented with taking some caffeine pills I got at CVS (I had a weird Saturday and quickly decided against it). I would have to rely on my own adrenaline. My first cousin, Pam Herbert, a doctor whose specialty is emergency medicine, was less than pleased with the dehydration part of the plan. She changed her schedule so she could sit up in the gallery above the Senate floor, right in front of me, and watch me like a hawk. She stayed there the entire time.

My other preparation was spiritual. I believe in the power of prayer and knew that I couldn't get through this challenge without some divine help. So beyond my own pastor, I also reached out to a number of family members and friends to ask for prayer. Some of the most moving prayers came from my three Senate Democrat colleagues who also grew up in the Black church—Senator Angela Alsobrooks from Maryland, Senator Lisa Blunt Rochester from Delaware, and Reverend Raphael Warnock from Georgia. We share a tradition, and we share a belief in the power of intercession and that *the prayers of the righteous availeth much.*[7] They are righteous people and truly were there for me. To this day, one of the most treasured moments I had on the Senate floor was in the minutes before I began; I was nervous and uncertain, and Lisa came up to me and asked if we could pray again. She laid her hands on me, prayed over me, and called on divine strength, wisdom, and guidance. I teared up and felt almost supercharged. And then, I was recognized by the presiding officer. I began speaking and said I would do so for as long as I was physically able.

Soon I began reading letters from our constituents. The notes, many handwritten, conveyed a palpable sense of fear. Fear not just of the difficult circumstances people were facing—whether that was living with a disability, a degenerative disease, or financial instability—but that any change to the programs they relied on would completely upend their lives.

One note, written on a piece of paper bearing the name of a charity, torn from the kind of notepad someone receives in exchange for a modest donation, read, "Hi, Senator Booker. Medicaid has saved my life many, many times. Without it, many people in America will die. Please help us."

"Please help us" was underlined multiple times.

Another, written in tiny, neat handwriting: "Dear Senator Booker, when I got out of the Navy, I had mental illness. I needed psychiatric medicine to stop going in and out of the hospital. Because of Medicaid, I have medicine that has kept me out of the hospital for 18 years. Without Medicaid and my medicine, I will wind up in the hospital."

A constituent who had worked for a local board of

education in New Jersey for twenty-five years and whose permanently disabled daughter relied on Medicaid to maintain her independence was terrified about threats to the programs her daughter relied on and threats to her own Social Security.

She ended her note with a simple plea: "We want to go to work, take care of our families, and ensure all citizens have the health services they deserve. . . . Please take action to defend and protect these programs."

A postcard sent from a small town in New Jersey asked, "Dear Senator Booker, I am writing to ask you if my Social Security is now in danger. Please let me know. It is very important to me. Thank you."

After reading letters from people in my home state on the floor of the Senate, I began to share stories of people from across the country who had also reached out to my office. I started to read out loud a letter from a woman named Kayanna Spooner who had written from Chippewa Falls, Wisconsin. She wrote,

> I am 63 years old. My husband Joe and I have five children and three grandchildren and live a wonderful life as our family is growing. We own businesses and work to contribute Social Security for ourselves and our employees. We did all the things we could do to secure our future and

> contribute to the larger community of those in need. We felt that we were living the American dream until one day in 2012 I was diagnosed with Parkinson's disease. Parkinson's disease is a degenerative brain disease that progresses over time.
>
> It is unrelenting and affects motor and nerve processes. Loss of benefits will have a direct and daily effect on me and my family as we navigate the medical needs we will be facing. I will need progressive and comprehensive care as I age. I will need medication every single day of my life, and I will need the security of a generous society to care for me. Millions of others join me there.
>
> Please Senator Booker, please protect my Social Security.

I had made it halfway through her letter when I stopped. A familiar heartbreak surfaced as I stood on the floor, and emotions I couldn't contain poured out of me. I choked up and felt connected to a person I had never met.

I thought about my dad's battle with Parkinson's and about my mom's pain, grief, and struggle to care for him. I thought about all the disease had taken from him and how much I missed my dad. And I thought about how scared our family was in the face of his diagnosis.

For those who live with Parkinson's or other debilitating, degenerative diseases, and for the people who love them, the disease lends itself to isolation and silent suffering. But Kayanna's courageous letter and those of so many others who spoke up about their intimate struggles were an implicit rejection of the idea that sharing their private pain and personal anguish somehow reflected weakness. They were defiant. They were taking back their agency. Sharing their testimonies of private suffering was an act of extraordinary strength and deliberate strategy.

"Vulnerability sounds like truth and feels like courage. Truth and courage aren't always comfortable, but they're never weakness," Brené Brown writes in her book *Daring Greatly*.[8] To be vulnerable is to exercise your power. At a time when many people feel most at risk, to speak up, to speak out, or to speak to your struggle is an act of taking back control.

Vulnerability ends isolation, builds new connections, and creates community. Communities can then better organize, advocate, and increase awareness. Communities can also defend, fight back, and even win against forces once more powerful than an individual, but not more powerful than a group or a movement.

At multiple points during my long speech, my body showed its limitations. My feet were numb, my muscles were cramping, and my legs grew weak. The carpet beneath my feet may have fared worse than me—by the time I was done speaking, it was worn up into balls that looked like tangled tumbleweeds. But in one of the most physically vulnerable points in my life, I found strength in community.

Dozens prepared me, wrote words that I read, counseled me (don't take caffeine pills!), prayed with me, and believed in me.

During the course of those twenty-five hours and five minutes, so many slipped me notes of strength and encouragement, stayed awake with me, watched over me, and lifted my spirit past my body's physical limitations. On multiple occasions, my staff scribbled the exact procedural language onto scraps of paper that they handed me that would allow me to take questions while continuing the effort: "I yield for a question while retaining the floor."

My friend Senator Chris Murphy of Connecticut agreed to be there for the duration of the speech. Hour after hour, he had my back, standing by me and supporting me on the floor. He coordinated with dozens of my Democratic colleagues who came to support me and give my voice a break by asking questions. Dozens of members of the House of Representatives came and filled the back of the chamber, from Democratic leader Hakeem Jeffries of New York to my colleagues in the New Jersey delegation, including my own congresswoman serving her first months in office, LaMonica McIver.

And so many Americans across our nation helped too, and their energy, their encouragement, and their belief came through as many millions viewed clips on social media, and countless people engaged in conversations about what they could do in this moment. And the more my physical strength emptied out, the more the Senate chamber filled up. The gallery above was full with hundreds and hundreds passing through during the twenty-five hours. I stepped out in faith, out of my comfort zone, beyond my perceived physical limits, and, exposed and vulnerable, I found I didn't stand alone.

After I reached the twenty-four-hour mark, knowing that I was approaching Strom Thurmond's record, I remarked that just steps from where I stood, there was a room in the Senate named after him. I had passed it often—sometimes with a sense of quiet triumph, sometimes with a deeper humility, knowing how many lives had been lost, how many battles had been fought and sacrifices made to make it possible for me and other Black senators to now serve in this chamber.

"There is a room here in the Senate named after Strom

Thurmond," I said. "To hate him is wrong. And maybe my ego got too caught up, thinking that if I stood here maybe—just maybe—I could break this record of the man who tried to stop the rights upon which I stand. I'm not here though because of his speech. I'm here despite his speech. I'm here because as powerful as he was, the people were more powerful."

In that moment, I remembered how I had started the speech the night before—by talking about my hero and friend, Congressman John Lewis. I had started by sharing his words—"Get in good trouble, necessary trouble, and help redeem the soul of America"—and asking myself what I was doing to live up to them. So, at the end, I returned to talking about John, and I shared the words he had once uttered to someone who had brutally beaten him amidst a nonviolent protest and years later sought his forgiveness: John Lewis forgave him, and then said to his son: "This nation needs you too." It was at that exact moment that Majority Leader Chuck Schumer stopped me to tell me the record had been broken. I only later learned that the words that broke Strom Thurmond's record for longest speech on the floor of the United States Senate were not my own—they were John Lewis's words of grace.

The chamber erupted in applause. The presiding officer called for order—but in a rare moment, he broke with Senate tradition and rules and allowed the ovation to continue. The gallery rose to its feet. That presiding officer was Senator John Curtis, a Republican from Utah, who just before taking the chair that hour, had crossed the aisle—literally—and handed me a note that said: "Don't stop. You can do this."

After my speech, I hugged my colleagues, went into the cloakroom, and ate a banana that Senator Peter Welch of Vermont—who is infinitely kind—had handed me as I left the floor. Maybe it was because I hadn't eaten in four days, but sitting down for the first time in twenty-five hours in the Senate Democratic Cloakroom (in what felt like the most comfortable chair in the mid-Atlantic region), eating that banana, surrounded by some of my extraordinary team, was one of the best meals I have ever had.

Our effort did not block or advance any legislation—there was no single bill that was responsible for this crisis and no single one that could fix it. Our goal was to lift up the voices and the courageous vulnerability of people from across New Jersey and across the country. We did so, and in turn, their courage was contagious. In the days and weeks following, my office was overwhelmed with tens of thousands of letters and calls from people wanting to share their stories. A few days after the speech, millions of people marched at Hands Off protests that had been scheduled across the country. I was moved by the photos and videos I received throughout the day of marchers who carried signs with quotes from my speech.

Amidst the tens of thousands of pieces of correspondence I received, one of the most powerful was a letter that read, in part,

> Many citizens feel alienated from the representatives who represent them. Many people whom I have spoken to are afraid and losing hope. . . . Filibustering was a brilliant strategic move, especially in contrast to Strom Thurmond's historical use of it 68 years ago to obstruct civil rights for Black Americans. As an African American Senator, your filibuster became a rallying cry for unity and compassion in a political landscape often marred by hatred and division.

The letter was from Wanda Williams-Bailey, the granddaughter of Senator Strom Thurmond. In 2003, Wanda's mother, Mrs. Essie Mae Washington-Williams, a Black woman, had powerfully revealed a secret she had long kept: Her father was Strom Thurmond.

Mrs. Washington-Williams said at a press conference at the time, "At this juncture in my life, I am looking for closure, I am not bitter. I am not angry. In fact, there is a great sense of peace that has come over me in the past year. Once I decided that I would no longer harbor such a great secret, that many others knew, I feel as though a tremendous weight has finally lifted. I am Essie Mae Washington-Williams, and at last, I feel completely free."[9]

* * *

OUR HISTORY is full of people who, amidst personal pain, fear, frustration, and injustice, harnessed the power of their vulnerability by transforming private struggles into public strength. They took risks, spoke out, and elevated the stories of others. And in doing so, they created movements that politicians and others could not ignore.

When the AIDS epidemic devastated our country, patients were shamed and blamed. They faced ignorance, ridicule, and discrimination. Many who died were buried without funerals; families, gripped by fear, hid the truth of their loved ones' deaths. The government refused to acknowledge the crisis for far too long. But courageous HIV-positive activists like Cleve Jones stepped forward. They spoke openly about their diagnoses and mourned publicly for their friends. And in one of the more powerful acts of defiant vulnerability, they began the NAMES Project AIDS Memorial Quilt—a living, growing memorial to those lost to AIDS. Through thousands of handmade patches, people shared names, memories, love, and loss. And when the quilt was unfolded across the National Mall, it forced Washington and the nation to face the truth. These activists inspired a nation to act.

Leaders who assert that vulnerability is weakness and that bluster is strength do so in an effort to minimize the power of others and assert their control. They try to shame, to embarrass, to force people into silence about their own pain and about any attempt to collectively address it. They deny others' struggles, disparage vulnerability, and suppress community as part of a strategy—they believe, for example, they can get away with giving tax cuts to the rich and powerful while eliminating the programs millions of vulnerable people rely on because they believe those people have no voice, no one will care, and their suffering will stay invisible. For such leaders, shared vulnerability is ultimately a threat. Their power depends on a world in which, even though people have common pain, they do not realize that they have common purpose, a world where people share in suffering but not in the struggle to end it.

Now more than ever, we need more people who will fight against attempts to distract, diminish, or disregard the struggles of others. We need more truth tellers, people willing to speak of their pain, flaws, and fears—and inspire others to do the same.

In this moral moment, we need those who show the fullness of their being—their brokenness and their endurance, their wounds and their healing, their mistakes and their search for growth and redemption. We need those who speak when silence feels safer. Who tell the defiant truth when obedience is rewarded. Who understand that real strength is not found in shallow swagger but in the depths of shared vulnerability.

We are those people.

And the power of the people is greater than the people in power.

* * *

A FEW DAYS after reading the letters from Kayanna and others on the Senate floor, I was holding a town hall in New Jersey when three people stood up to speak. A mother, Chris Peters, introduced her son Joseph, who stood quietly next to her, holding his notebook. With love and great pride, she shared that Joseph, who has autism, had been living independently in his own apartment for seven years and that the only reason he could live in that apartment with the help of an aide was because of the support he received from Medicaid. "This is Medicaid at work," she said of her son. She was extremely scared about what any cut to services would mean for Joseph and for so many others. "I don't sleep now," she said. "What am I going to do if anything happens, how am I going to maintain his life that we worked so hard to get? It's no way to live, but I will do everything in my power and anything I can to support you and anybody that can make this not happen."

She had started by saying that Joseph "has a lot of anxiety, and this is really overwhelming for him," but that he wanted to be there. In a room full of hundreds of people, where most would have a difficult time speaking about their private fears and struggles, this young man with admitted anxiety stepped forward and began reading from his notebook: "I just want to say, I love my helpers, for one thing, I love my apartment, and just please, please, for the love of God, don't cut Medicaid."

When he finished reading, the room erupted into applause, and soon everyone was standing.

Then, Joseph's helper, Martin, stepped forward too. He shared, "I have to say it has been a pleasure working with this young man. . . . I am part of the working poor—I was, until I met this family, and they took care of me, and now I take care of them. Please, anything I can do, I will do."

Chris, Joseph, and Martin created a chain reaction—a thousand strangers entered a gymnasium, and after the three of them spoke, the room was ignited. Hearts opened, connections were made, and a community with a greater shared purpose was created. This was so much more than a discussion of policy. A young man, who many might see as powerless, showed all of us the power he had—by taking a risk, stepping forward, and opening up.

My dad, just like he was in that movie theater bathroom, would have been beaming.

3

PATRIOTISM

O, yes,
I say it plain,
America never was America to me,
And yet I swear this oath—
America will be!

—Langston Hughes,
"Let America Be America Again"

"HAS YOU GOT ONE OF DEM OLE FLAGS TO SPARE? We'd like to have one, sah!"[1] It was early morning, May 13, 1862. The *Planter*, a Confederate ship, now floated beside the USS *Onward* off the coast of South Carolina.[2] The question had come, improbably, from a group of people who had just escaped slavery, people who, only moments earlier, had risked being blasted out of the water by both Confederate and Union cannons. And yet, their first request after reaching safety was to replace their white flag of surrender with the American flag.[3]

Their journey had begun hours earlier, in the dead of night, when a twenty-three-year-old enslaved man named Robert Smalls launched an audacious plan to secure freedom for himself, his family, and over a dozen others. Smalls had served as an enslaved crewmember of the *Planter* working under the supervision of three white officers. He studied how to navigate Charleston's complex harbor, memorized Confederate signals, tracked munitions transported on the ship, and paid close attention to the captain's routines and mannerisms—including his habit of wearing a large straw hat as he moved the ship through Confederate checkpoints.[4]

In the early hours of May 13, while the white officers slept ashore, Smalls, wearing the captain's coat and his large straw hat tipped low over his head, took command of the *Planter*—loaded with Confederate weapons—and slipped it from its mooring. He picked up his family and others waiting at a wharf upriver, then sailed the *Planter* straight into danger.[5] The plan was incredibly risky: The *Planter* needed to pass by four Confederate forts, each equipped with weapons that could destroy the ship instantly. At each checkpoint, Smalls mimicked the captain's posture and demeanor with precision.

A House Committee on Naval Affairs report later provided these details: "Approaching Fort Sumter, Smalls stood in the pilot-house leaning out of the window with his arms folded across his breast, after the manner of Captain Relay [*sic*], the commander of the boat, and his head covered with the huge straw hat which Captain Relyea commonly wore on such occasions. The signal required to be given by all steamers passing out was blown as cooly as if General Ripley [who was responsible for Charleston's defenses] was on board going out on a tour of inspection."[6]

After 4:15 AM, a Confederate sentry at Fort Sumter waved him through.[7] By the time Confederate forces realized that the ship was moving toward Union lines, it was too late.[8] The *Planter* was out of range—but not out of danger.

The captain of the nearest Union ship, the *Onward*, saw the *Planter* quickly approaching. Fearing it could be a Confederate attack, Captain John Nickels sounded the alarm and ordered his crew to aim the cannons at the approaching ship. But at the last moment, he saw that it was flying a white flag—a bedsheet that had been raised by Smalls and his crew.[9]

Smalls called out to Nickels across the water, "Good morning, sir! I have brought you some of the old United States' guns, sir!"[10] Then came the request from those aboard the *Planter*: an American flag of their own.[11]

Smalls and the *Planter*'s crew were inducted into the Union army the very next day. His heroics made national headlines. Although Black Americans were barred from military service at the time, his booming celebrity and extraordinary heroism forced an exception. Smalls used that spotlight to lobby President Lincoln and Secretary of War Edwin Stanton to allow Black enlistment. Just three months after commandeering the *Planter*, Smalls helped secure the first official authorization for Black troops to join the Union cause.[12]

Over the course of the war, Smalls fought in at least seventeen naval battles. In most, he continued to serve as pilot of the *Planter*.[13] In one battle, the *Planter*'s then-captain, a white Union officer, ordered Smalls to surrender the ship to Confederate forces. Smalls refused. He knew that after capture, the white officers would be treated with respect as prisoners of war, but he and his Black crewmates would almost certainly face torture, reenslavement, or death. As professor and sociologist Andrew Billingsley recounts in his extraordinary book, *Yearning to Breathe Free*, Smalls snapped, "Not by a damn sight will I beach this boat." When the captain retreated to the coal bunker, Smalls locked him inside, took full command, and piloted the ship safely back to Union territory. He was promoted that day, becoming the first Black man to captain a US Navy vessel.[14]

Smalls's heroics extended beyond his military service. While the *Planter* was undergoing repairs in Philadelphia during the war, Smalls was arrested for riding a whites-only streetcar. When word spread that the hero of the *Planter*, a decorated Union captain, had been so brazenly dishonored, it sparked a boycott that led to the eventual desegregation of Philadelphia's transit system.[15] After the war, Smalls served as a delegate at the South Carolina Constitutional Convention, where he helped write the state's new constitution, successfully proposing that the state of South Carolina create its first free system of public education.[16]

Smalls served five terms in Congress, representing South Carolina's Seventh District. He was an effective advocate for his state, but even then, his own life mirrored the fragility of American progress: not always linear, not without setbacks, and subject to periods of brutal backlash. In one bitter chapter, Congressman Smalls was arrested, tried, and convicted on false bribery charges—a political hit job orchestrated by white Democrats eager to silence him. And in another indignity, after serving twenty years as the US customs collector for the Port of Beaufort, his own senators blocked his reappointment and ended his service.[17]

Robert Smalls had risked everything. At any point, he had earned the right to rest, and it would have been justified if he became disillusioned. He spent twenty-three years enslaved. He seized a valuable Confederate ship and delivered it to the Union. He volunteered to fight for a nation that refused to let Black Americans enlist. He served in elected office. He launched public schools. He helped desegregate public transportation nearly a century before Freedom Riders in the 1960s would continue the work. He was a patriot not only in word but in sacrifice and deed.

And still, he endured the backlash and the betrayal of the very ideals he'd fought for. He watched Reconstruction collapse under a wave of racial terror. He saw white supremacists reclaim the South through violence and watched Black Americans stripped of their vote, beaten, and lynched. He was slandered, falsely convicted, and pushed from public service. The nation he loved fell far short of his aspirations for it.

And yet, Robert Smalls never gave up. He never stopped fighting. He never stopped believing that America could be better, would one day be better. He knew that the road toward progress was hard and that the road to justice was long, and through his own experiences, he knew that even great advances could be bitterly lost. And yet for him, in military battle and in his fight for America, surrender was never an option—you always fight on.

He died at the age of seventy-five in a home he owned in Beaufort, South Carolina. It was the same house he had grown up in, the same house where he had been enslaved.[18]

A home that was once a place of bondage was now a testament to his liberation, to his devotion to, and faith in, the unfinished promise of America.

* * *

I WORRY ABOUT those who use our country's sacred symbols to undermine everything they represent, those who seek to hide their hypocrisy and obscure injustice by wrapping them in the American flag. This dangerous manipulation of patriotism mistakes cheap branding for deep belonging. It seeks to divide Americans into camps of loyal and disloyal, "us" and "them." It confuses dissent with treason, constructive criticism with betrayal. Our patriotic symbols that should unite us become swords to threaten and bully, to demand conformity or silence opposition.

This is not new. Throughout our history, patriotism has been distorted for hate and power. In the 1930s, Father Charles Coughlin, whose radio show once counted nearly a third of the country as its audience, sought to advance a fear-fueled, antidemocratic, antisemitic, anti-immigrant, and fundamentally un-American worldview. He wrapped his hatred in counterfeit patriotism, imploring his followers to "rise in your places and pledge with me to restore America for the Americans."[19]

In the 1950s, Senator Joseph McCarthy branded suspicion and paranoia as "Americanism with its sleeves rolled."[20] Using the power of his office, he launched unsubstantiated public attacks and investigations into his perceived political enemies—ranging from other elected officials to university professors to artists and journalists. Cloaked in the language of liberty, he tried to convince Americans that he alone could protect them from whatever they feared most.

In our own time, we have seen a false patriotism turned into a presidential loyalty test, with our flag literally being turned into a weapon. On January 6, 2021, rioters carried it into the halls of Congress not as a banner of unity but as a tool of assault against both patriotic police officers and our patriotic ideals. They tried to overturn an election; to halt the peaceful transfer of power; and then, in one final act of moral inversion, the president they sought to illegitimately reinstall called them "patriots" and pardoned them from their criminal convictions.

I am deeply disturbed by this manipulation of patriotism.

But I also worry about those who would walk away from American patriotism because others have wielded its distortion as a weapon.

I believe patriotism at its best is a devotion to shared ideals and a devotion to one another. It shows up in many forms of service. There is a quiet nobility to patriotism.

A firm resolve that doesn't advertise or seek acclaim. It is humble, self-interrogating, seen less in single acts than in consistent striving. Patriotism is what drives a person to serve in the military; it's what inspires a firefighter to charge into a burning building to save a child; motivates a nonviolent protester to sit at a lunch counter knowing they will get beaten; or moves a person to take off work, get someone to watch their kids, travel hours to go to their state's or our nation's capital, and appeal to their representatives for a law that will protect their children and others. This patriotic devotion is the yearning to make a better society, a better nation; it's a call to serve.

Patriotism does not believe that our country is without fault or cannot be improved, or that efforts to draw attention to our failings undermine us. In fact, patriotism criticizes relentlessly as necessary. As James Baldwin said, "I love America more than any other country in the world, and, exactly for this reason, I insist on the right to criticize her perpetually."[21] With this kind of devotion comes an assumed responsibility: This is wrong *and* I will lend my efforts, make my sacrifice, and devote my spirit to change it.

Throughout our history, it has often been the people who had the least reason to believe in America's promises who fought the hardest to make those promises real. They met the distortion of America's ideals and symbols not only with their disapproval but with their fervent devotion.

After Robert Smalls risked everything to free himself and his family, he immediately dedicated his life to the possibility of a freer nation. He wanted to serve proudly under the American flag at the same time as he was striving to redeem it.

Suffragists marched proudly with American flags as they sought to challenge America to live up to its ideals. Susan B. Anthony, a fierce critic of America's shortcomings, marched for women's suffrage with American flags waving, proclaiming, "It was we, the people; not we, the white male citizens; nor yet we, the male citizens; but we, the whole people, who formed the Union. And we formed it, not to give the blessings of liberty, but to secure them; not to the half of ourselves and the half of our posterity, but to the whole people—women as well as men."[22] Mary Ann Shadd Cary, a suffragist and teacher who was forced to flee to Canada for helping enslaved people escape along the Underground Railroad, returned to the United States during the Civil War to help recruit soldiers for the Union army. She defiantly declared, "The crowning glory of American citizenship is that it may be shared equally by people of every nationality, complexion, and sex."[23]

Native Americans, who had endured unspeakable horrors at the hands of the American government, likewise rose in overwhelming numbers to fight for the United States and defeat fascism during World War II. To this day, Native Americans continue serving in the military at higher rates than any other group.[24]

A seventeen-year-old Japanese American named Daniel Inouye, who was deemed an "enemy alien" when the United States entered World War II and was denied entry into the military, petitioned the government to fight for the United States. When he was finally allowed to enlist, he joined other Japanese American soldiers serving in a segregated unit. During one offensive in Italy, Inouye was on the verge of throwing a grenade when he was struck by a German grenade that severed his right hand from his body. Reaching with his left hand, he retrieved the unexploded grenade from his severed hand's grasp and threw it at the Germans.[25] He lost his entire arm. His sacrifice inspired a nation, and he went on to serve as a senator from Hawaii for nearly five decades.

I sometimes meet people who tell me that they feel like the flag doesn't belong to them—that it has been claimed by those who use it to distort the ideals of America, who use it to represent partisan goals rather than shared purpose. I find this disturbing, and I hope you do too. I believe it is time for more people to take responsibility for reclaiming the ideal of patriotism—and with it, our nation's flag, symbols, and songs. I believe we must reassert our pride in the bold ideals of America and our devotion to making those ideals real. If generations before us could put forth their faith in our nation amid hatred, exclusion, or extraordinary hardship—if they could claim the hope of America in defiance of those who betrayed it—then who are we to abandon it now?

* * *

WHEN I was twenty-three years old and preparing to move to England to start my Rhodes Scholarship, a friend recommended that I meet with Senator Bill Bradley, a Rhodes Scholar, who, in addition to being my home-state senator, was a former NBA champion. I traveled to his Washington, DC, office to meet with him (in the same building where my office is now), and I was immediately in awe. I couldn't believe that someone of his stature was taking time to sit with me. But from that very first meeting, Bill became a sounding board, a counselor, and a kind of moral North Star.

For three decades, he has challenged me to cultivate a humble, serious reverence for public service and an unflinching love for others—all others. Especially, he said, the ones who don't agree with you. Doing the difficult work of advancing shared ideals and common cause across divides is, to him, the embodiment of patriotism.

When I joined the Senate, he offered me a piece of

advice that I took to heart: Take time to get to know your Republican colleagues. Invite them to share a meal, or at least go to their offices. Ask them about their lives. Learn about their families, their ideas, their reasons for being in the Senate. Ask for their counsel. And when they give it, really listen.

So, I did. It became something of a personal odyssey to fulfill Bill's instruction and try to meet with every one of my Republican colleagues. I learned so much from the early conversations I had, and I soon established relationships that helped me get things done—solve problems for my constituents, pass bills, and speak on issues that matter with a bipartisan voice. I also found great personal enrichment from developing some friendships with colleagues across the aisle.

There was one Republican senator in particular whom everyone spoke of with a profound reverence. He was a lion of the Senate, a man who commanded attention and earned deep respect. Many also spoke of his temper. One senator told me, "You're not really a full senator until John McCain has chewed you out."

Not necessarily with the hope of fulfilling that particular bucket list item, I tried to arrange a meeting with Senator McCain. Getting on to his schedule was difficult; he was busy, and understandably so. When his staff finally gave me a meeting, I arrived at his office a little nervous and, admittedly, a little disappointed. I'd been told I'd only get fifteen minutes to speak with him. At least, I thought, there was barely enough time for me to say something stupid and set him off.

Senator McCain welcomed me into his office with a graciousness that caught me off guard. Before we even sat down, he took me on a walk around the room, pointing out photographs on his walls of family, fellow Americans, and world leaders whom he had met.

I asked questions, a lot of them, and he responded generously with a mix of humor, candor, and reflection. Any stiffness between us melted away almost immediately. I felt like I was sitting where I had once sat with Senator Bill Bradley decades before, a young man being mentored by a generous elder statesman. I was sitting across from someone who had struggled mightily to serve his country and had the wisdom to show for his struggles.

As we talked, he opened up about his life with a kind of unflinching vulnerability that I wasn't expecting. He pulled out folders and photographs from his time as a Navy aviator and documents from his five and a half years as a prisoner of war in Vietnam.[26] These weren't casual mementos. He held them with reverence, almost as if they were sacred artifacts. I'll never forget how he showed me the photo—not even the original, I don't think—of his broken body being pulled from a lake in Hanoi after the wing of his jet had been blown off. But it wasn't the image itself that moved me, it was the way he held it, as if cradling something fragile, as if holding a memory that was still fresh, one that still gave him pain and purpose. He told me how, a year into his captivity, the Vietnamese discovered that his father was an admiral in the US Navy and offered to release him. He refused. Accepting an early release while his fellow prisoners remained would have violated the code of honor: first captured, first released.[27] He chose honor and solidarity over even his own survival. As he spoke about those years, the darkness, the isolation, the pain, he grew emotional. And so did I.

He told me that in that prison camp, stripped of everything, his love for America grew deeper. His reverence for our national ideals—freedom, dignity, shared sacrifice—only intensified. He said that when everything else is burned away, what remains is what you love. To me, it was clear: He loved his country and he loved his fellow Americans.

John told me the story of a fellow POW, Mike Christian, from near Selma, Alabama. It was a story I would later return to and reread in his speeches after John passed. Mike had stitched an American flag on his shirt using a bamboo needle and scraps of colored cloth the POWs had pooled together. Every day, they would hang it and say the Pledge of Allegiance. One day, the Vietnamese guards discovered the flag. They beat Mike brutally. Hours later, as the guards slept, McCain awoke to see that Mike was back in the corner—bruised and bloodied, his eyes nearly swollen shut—stitching another flag. In a speech at the 1988 Republican National Convention, John said, "He was not making that flag because it made Mike Christian feel better. He was making that flag because he knew how important it was for us to be able to pledge our allegiance to our flag and our country."[28]

We spoke for well over an hour that day. More than once, when staff came in to signal that time was up, he waved them away with a sharp "Not yet." At the end of our meeting, John turned serious. He told me that there are two kinds of senators: politicians and statesmen. "The Senate," he said, "has enough politicians—about eighty of them, by my count." Then he looked at me hard and repeated it twice, with force: "Be a statesman. Be a statesman. This country needs more statesmen."

He spoke with anguish about the rise of tribalism, the zero-sum partisanship that pits Americans against each other and replaces shared purpose with endless division that is all too often false and opportunistic. He challenged me to practice a patriotism rooted not in party but in principle. He didn't hold himself up as a perfect paragon of this virtue either. He was deeply candid about his own flaws. He had come up short at times, he admitted. But at his best, he led this way.

I got to see that kind of leadership from him firsthand—and often. From that first meeting grew a friendship that lasted until his death. I visited him at his ranch in Arizona for conferences and treasured our long conversations. I traveled abroad with him on my first congressional delegation trip, which was to a global security conference in Munich, Germany. I will never forget how determined he was in helping me ensure the passage of appropriations protecting rehabilitative services for veterans with traumatic brain injuries in New Jersey and across the country.

But perhaps no moment demonstrates more the kind of patriotism he had urged me to embody than what happened in the summer of 2017. John had opposed the Affordable Care Act (ACA) from the beginning, as did his entire party. Repealing it became a rallying cry for many Republicans on the campaign trail. But when they gained control of the Senate and repeal was finally on the table—with nothing to replace it—Senator McCain faced a choice. Repealing the ACA would strip health coverage from tens of millions of Americans. Voting to save the ACA would anger many in his own party, including its leader, Donald Trump.

John had returned to the Senate for the first time since announcing that he was battling terminal brain cancer, and after days of deliberation, the final vote began after midnight on July 28. As his Republican colleagues paced around him, he spoke with Vice President Pence on the floor for twenty minutes before taking a call from President Trump outside the chamber.[29] At 1:28 AM, he reentered the chamber. At 1:29, he approached the dais and stretched out his once shattered arm. After holding it there for a moment, during which everyone on both sides of the aisle seemed to be holding their breath in anticipation, he gave a thumbs-down as he declared "no."

He was the deciding vote. He stood with every Democrat and just two other Republicans—Susan Collins from Maine and Lisa Murkowski from Alaska—and in doing so, he saved healthcare for millions of Americans.

In what would be Senator McCain's final speech on the floor of the United States Senate, he offered a moral clarity that still echoes: "I hope we can again rely on humility, on our need to cooperate, on our dependence on each other to learn how to trust each other again and by so doing better serve the people who elected us. Stop listening to the bombastic loudmouths on the radio and television and the internet. To hell with them. They don't want anything done for the public good. Our incapacity is their livelihood."[30]

John McCain demonstrated to all of us that real patriotism isn't always loud, but it is always loyal. Loyal to ideals, loyal to country, loyal to people—even, and especially, those with whom you disagree. Patriotism is about standing for something bigger than yourself. Standing even when it's hard. Standing even when you stand alone.

* * *

THREE DECADES after I first met Senator Bradley in his Senate office, I was sitting in the audience, listening to him speak, when he paused. He was performing a one-man show he had written, *Rolling Along: An American Story*. It was the end of the show, and he was talking about the last time he had been in Crystal City, Missouri, the small town that had raised and shaped him. He said he was surprised by how much things had changed—the factory had been torn down, stores on the town's main street sat vacant. Until, he said, he went to the Mississippi River. "And there it was," Bill said, "as it always had been. Moving. Silent. Powerful. Giving things. Taking things away." He then went on to offer what I believe is one of the best definitions of patriotism I have ever heard: "Take responsibility for yourself. Respect your fellow human being. Disagree with them honestly and civilly. Enjoy their humanity. And never look down on people you don't understand. If enough of us do those things, then America, like the mighty Mississippi, will just keep rolling along."[31]

This is the patriotism that asks us to be of service, to stand up for our own rights and the rights of others, to lend a hand, to protect the weak, to help, to heal, to repair, and to strengthen community. It draws people in and doesn't push people out. It demands we be proud of our nation's promise, even as we hold it accountable for its imperfections. This is the patriotism that made an escaped slave ask for the flag of the country that had enslaved him. The patriotism that fueled suffragists, civil rights activists, soldiers, and seekers of justice across generations. It is not passive. It is work. It is service. It is sacrifice.

Now, as much as ever, our country needs committed patriots who love it enough to work for, fight for, and insist on its improvement. We need patriots who name what is wrong, acknowledge injustice—get outraged, even—but then get out working. Our devotion should make us deeply proud of our country—we are all inheritors of a legacy of patriots. Our country's anthem, our Pledge of Allegiance, and all things red, white, and blue don't belong to some, they can't be co-opted or captured by any faction, party, or opportunist. The American flag belongs to us, all of us. This nation is our shared privilege and our collective responsibility. Our flag, our anthem, and our ideals are the call of a country to its people to stand together and strive together, to put forth the best measure of our devotion in service of our nation.

* * *

THE AMERICAN flag had finally been raised above the *Planter* when Hannah Smalls, Robert's wife, emerged from belowdecks with her children.

Free for the first time in her life, standing on the upper deck of the ship, Hannah lifted her infant son above her head, toward the flag, and said, "Just look up dare, honey! it'll do you good, I knows it will."[32]

A decade later, with the war over and the possibility of a healed country before them, Robert and Hannah's daughter Elizabeth stepped onto another deck, this one on the second-story veranda above Beaufort's Bay Street.[33] It was the Fourth of July, and amidst a townwide celebration filled with music, parades, and speeches, Elizabeth had a special task: to read the Declaration of Independence to the crowd that had gathered.[34] Elizabeth, who had been born into slavery, read the words of our founders, declaring that "all men are created equal." As Cate Lineberry wrote in *Be Free or Die*, her "reading was the highlight of the day, as most of the adults in the audience had once been enslaved and could not read or write."[35] The excitement generated by Elizabeth's reading of the Declaration of Independence that day was not because its promises had been fulfilled but because those gathered believed they could be.

The final words Elizabeth would have read that day, the final words of the Declaration of Independence, are a simple but profound declaration of devotion: "We mutually pledge to each other our Lives, our Fortunes, and our sacred Honor."

I believe our founders knew the only way our nation was going to survive and thrive was if we lived that ideal—a devotion not just to our country but to one another. A devotion that demands humility, demands sacrifice and service, and demands, even amidst political divides, that we remember our patriotic duty to honor one another.

4

TRUTH

Somebody's asking . . . "How long will justice be crucified, and truth bear it?"
I come to say to you this afternoon, however difficult the moment, however frustrating the hour, it will not be long, because "truth crushed to earth will rise again."

—Dr. Martin Luther King Jr.,
"How Long? Not Long," March 25, 1965

MOST NEW SENATORS ARE SWORN IN ON JANUARY 3 at the start of a Congress as part of an incoming class. There's a formal ceremony, an orientation, and a host of hand-holding to ease you into the job. But things for me were a little different—I'd arrived by special election, so I was coming in on my own. No class. No group orientation. Few instructions. Just me, standing alone on the Senate floor with my hand on a Bible—on Halloween, no less—taking the oath before the vice president.

I took my oath, shook many hands, and before the echoes of "congratulations!" had even faded, the Senate snapped back into business as usual.

First up: a confirmation vote for Congressman Mel Watt to lead the Federal Housing Finance Agency.[1] My staff had briefed me on the nomination, which seemed straightforward. But amid the flurry of backslaps, bear hugs, and big grins, I almost missed the start of the vote. Then—cutting through the buzz—I heard my name ring out across the chamber: "Senator Booker?"

A hush fell.

The entire Senate floor turned toward me. The gallery above—filled with my family, friends, and supporters—leaned forward. Their guy was about to cast his very first vote.

I froze.

While I'd been briefed on the nominee, I remained ignorant on an important question. How do you actually vote as a senator? Was there a secret button under the desk? A ceremonial lever? Some hidden switch—left for yes, right for no? It felt like stepping into a high-stakes escape room with no instructions. My degrees in political science, law, and history hadn't covered this part. I stood there like a kid who hadn't done the reading, glancing left and right, hoping to copy someone else's answer. Time stretched. My pulse quickened. I could feel the collective anticipation tightening around me like a necktie that's been pulled too tight.

Then, salvation: A colleague leaned over with the calm air of a seasoned pro and whispered, "Just raise your hand and say aye."

I followed the instructions, hand raised, voice steady—"Aye."

The chamber erupted in laughter. Some of my colleagues clapped. The gallery above, packed with family and friends who had traveled to witness this moment, burst into smiles. My first vote: cast. My first lesson: learned. Welcome to the United States Senate.

As I stood there casting my first vote, I knew I wasn't alone. *You are your ancestors' wildest dreams.* I have heard that aphorism many times, and I repeat it often to others of all backgrounds. But in that moment, I truly felt it. I felt the spirit of generations around me: my parents, my grandparents, my ancestors. I thought about the larger American struggle, the legion of activists from so many communities who elevated and overcame.

I thought about the trailblazers who had come before me. Mel Watt—the man I had just voted to confirm—was one of those trailblazers. In 1992, he and Congresswoman Eva Clayton became the first Black members of Congress from North Carolina in nearly a century. The last before them had been George Henry White, elected in 1898.[2]

Most Americans don't know much about George Henry White, a man from North Carolina who also helped found a community in New Jersey named in his honor (Whitesboro).[3] And that's a shame—his extraordinary story, his truth, deserve to be remembered.

George Henry White holds a singular place in American history. He was the last Black member of Congress elected from North Carolina in the nineteenth century—and, after the collapse of Reconstruction, the last Black American from the South to serve in Congress for nearly seven decades. His tenure marked both the promise of an emerging multiracial democracy and the fierce backlash that rose to destroy it.

After the Civil War, during the hopeful but fragile period of Reconstruction, Black political leadership flourished in the South. Formerly enslaved people, Union veterans, educators, and other men of immense courage, stature, and vision began to hold public office. Sixteen Black Americans served in Congress during the height of this era, and hundreds more were elected to state legislatures. They helped write new constitutions, expand voting rights, and establish the first public school systems in many Southern states.[4]

But this surge of Black political power was met with

white supremacist terror. Groups like the Ku Klux Klan launched systematic campaigns of violence and intimidation. As the Equal Justice Initiative has documented, more than two thousand Black men, women, and children were lynched during the twelve years of Reconstruction alone.[5] What Reconstruction built, white supremacists desperately sought to dismantle.

That dismantling accelerated in 1877, when a contested presidential election was resolved by a backroom compromise: Republican Rutherford B. Hayes would become president, and the last federal troops would be withdrawn from the South. Reconstruction was abandoned. In its place came voter suppression, racial violence, and the steady erasure of Black political representation.

Remarkably, in 1898, George Henry White was reelected to Congress from North Carolina's Second District. In the 1890s, a coalition of Black and white Republicans and white Populists, called the Fusion movement, had gained political power across the state. In 1896, they helped get Daniel L. Russell elected as governor and expanded voting rights, threatening the political dominance of the white Democratic establishment.[6] In response, Democrats waged a ruthless campaign in the 1898 election, employing racist propaganda, ballot manipulation, and threats of violence. And they won elections across the state.[7]

Their sweeping victories set the stage for a violent coup.

Just two days after White's reelection, North Carolina would become the site of one of the most chilling acts of racial violence in American history: the Wilmington massacre.[8]

On November 10, 1898, a mob of over five hundred armed white men stormed into Wilmington, North Carolina.[9] They began their violence by burning the offices of the *Daily Record*, the city's Black-owned newspaper. Its editor, Alexander Manly, had published an editorial rejecting racist lies being spread by Rebecca Felton, a former slave owner and public speaker who used her speeches to spread false allegations about Black men assaulting white women, inciting white men to violence. In one infamous speech, she said, "If it needs lynching to protect woman's dearest possession from the ravening human beasts—then I say lynch, a thousand times a week if necessary."[10] Two decades later, Rebecca Felton would go on to become the first woman to serve in the United States Senate.

White newspapers reprinted the *Daily Record*'s response to Felton's lies and hate speech, calling the *Record*'s editorial "vile" and "an insult to white womanhood."[11] It became the pretext for bloodshed.

A well-armed mob laid siege to Wilmington's Black community. The mob murdered Black residents and torched Black-owned businesses and homes. The estimates of those slaughtered were never accurately reported, ranging anywhere from thirty to three hundred. Thousands were forced to flee into the swamps surrounding the city, and many never returned. The Reverend J. Allen Kirk, the pastor at the Central Baptist Church and a Black leader in Wilmington, described the scene: "The shrieks and screams of children, of mothers, of wives were heard, such as caused the blood of the most inhuman person to creep. Thousands of women, children and men rushed to the swamps and there lay upon the earth in the cold to freeze and starve. The woods were filled with colored people. The streets were dotted with their dead bodies."[12]

At gunpoint, the mob forced Wilmington's mayor and city council to resign. They installed white supremacists in their place. It remains the only successful coup d'état in our country's history.[13] Among those forced to flee was Alexander Manly, the *Daily Record*'s editor.[14] He and his brother escaped to Washington, DC, where Congressman George Henry White reportedly sheltered them.[15] Outraged, White spent the next year speaking out across the country and into Canada, exposing the truth of the Wilmington massacre even as the press buried it under false headlines: "BLACKS PROVOKE TROUBLE" and "NEGROES, IT IS SAID, FIRED FIRST."[16]

The North Carolina legislature moved quickly to

amend the state constitution to once again disenfranchise Black voters.[17] Congressman White's loss was all but guaranteed by their efforts, and he chose not to run for reelection.[18]

But in January 1900, with his own political fate sealed by the violent terror of white supremacy, George Henry White introduced the first bill in US history to make lynching a federal crime.[19]

The following year, on January 29, 1901, George Henry White delivered his final speech before Congress. He stood alone—the last Black member of the House or Senate. He condemned the epidemic of lynching in America and warned that this "evil peculiar to America, yes, to the United States . . . must be met somehow, some day."[20] Then, with a tone both mournful and defiant, he began his conclusion: "This, Mr. Chairman, is perhaps the Negroes' temporary farewell to the American Congress. But let me say, phoenix-like he will rise up some day and come again. These parting words are in behalf of an outraged, heartbroken, bruised, and bleeding, but God-fearing people—faithful, industrious, loyal people—rising people, full of potential force."

With that, Black political representation vanished from Congress for nearly thirty years. And it would be the last time a Black person from the South would serve in Congress for more than seventy years.

And though more than two hundred bills to make lynching a federal crime would be introduced over the next 120 years—not one would pass.

* * *

THERE IS still so much painful truth buried in American soil.

In April 2018, I traveled to Montgomery, Alabama, for the opening of the National Memorial for Peace and Justice. Created by the Equal Justice Initiative under the extraordinary leadership of Bryan Stevenson, the memorial honors the thousands of Black Americans who were tortured and murdered in acts of racial terror—many in the dark of night, some in broad daylight, the perpetrators never held accountable.

At the heart of the memorial, 805 steel columns shaped like coffins are suspended from the ceiling—one for each county in America where a lynching occurred. Etched into each column are the names of the victims we know. The Equal Justice Initiative meticulously documented more than four thousand racial terror lynchings between 1877 and 1950.[21] Yet until this memorial opened, no national monument had recognized this epidemic of violence.

When you walk through it, your body feels the weight. You begin on level ground, face-to-face with the steel columns. Then the path descends. As you move deeper, the columns rise above you, suspended like bodies overhead. It's chilling. The air itself feels thick with grief and sadness and yet you also feel a sense of gratitude as names once violently and deliberately erased are lifted in a manner in which we can no longer look away. On the walls are the stories—grotesque, brutal, unforgettable. At one point, I saw a family sitting at one of the columns, quietly weeping, arms around one another. I didn't want to intrude. I walked on to the opening ceremony.

Bryan Stevenson spoke with singular moral power. He told us that as part of the memorial project, they had collected soil from lynching sites across the country. "We believe that in the soil there is the sweat of those who were enslaved," he said. "In the soil is the blood of those who were lynched. In the soil are the tears of those who were humiliated during segregation. But in the soil we have collected, we can plant something. And it can grow."[22]

Bryan has also shared the story of a Black woman who traveled to a remote site where a lynching had occurred to collect soil for the project. She was worried about going there by herself, but she went. Before she began digging, a white man drove by in his truck, slowed down and looked at her, and then turned around, parked his car, and got out. He walked up to her and asked what she was doing. She was nervous. She hesitated to tell him why she was there, but she did. According to Bryan, she said, "I'm digging soil because this is where a black man was lynched in 1931, and I'm going to honor his life."[23]

The woman had a piece of paper with her that explained the project. The man read her paper. And then he asked if he could join her.

He threw his hands into the dirt and began digging alongside her. The woman was so moved she began crying. As they finished filling the jar with dirt, she noticed that the man was shaking, and there were tears streaming down his face too.

She asked if he was OK.

The man looked at her and said he was worried—he was worried that it could have been his grandparents who had participated in this lynching.

"Now, beautiful things like that don't always happen when you tell the truth about history, when you try to actually look for redemption and restoration, when you have every reason to be afraid and angry," Bryan shared in an NPR interview. "But until we commit to some acts like that, until we tell the truth, we deny ourselves the beauty of redemption, the beauty of restoration."[24]

After the ceremony, I walked back through the memorial, under the heavy-hanging steel boxes. I noticed that the family who had been crying together earlier was still sitting there. It had been hours. I walked over to them and we began to talk. They shared that they were there not just for the opening of the memorial; their family member's name was etched into one of the steel boxes. For the first time, there had been a recognition of what had happened, of the horror and the crime, of what had been stolen from their family. For the first time, there, hanging in front of everyone, was the truth.

* * *

WE NEED to remind ourselves, today, that we tell the truth about our history not to humiliate our country but to heal it. There is great instruction, wisdom, and inspiration in our history. We elevate our own power when we celebrate the power of those who persevered, those who overcame injustice and, through great hardship, advanced our democracy.

We are not a lesser nation because we admit to injustice, we are a greater nation because courageous Americans from all backgrounds stood up to end those injustices, tell the truth, and confront wrongs. However painfully, Americans fought back and strode forward.

That is why I am not surprised that we currently see a president and politicians across the country who are trying to erase not only the wretchedness many of our ancestors faced, but also the heroism with which they faced it. Controlling how we understand our history is a powerful tool in the hands of those who wish to exert their control over the American people. They don't want to celebrate the people who were defiant against abuses of power; they don't want to elevate those who stood against the ugliness, confronted hate, and expanded democratic inclusion.

The banning of books and the scrubbing of knowledge of who we are and who we were from our classrooms and museums is not just an attempt to rewrite history, it is an attempt to erase the stories of those extraordinary people who shaped it. "They are acts of erasure—coordinated, sneaky attempts to cherry-pick our shared stories and decide who matters, censor our classrooms, and strip our communities of the places we go to learn, to connect, and to remember," wrote the leaders of the American Alliance of Museums, the League of Women Voters of the United States, and EveryLibrary in an open letter published in *Newsweek* in April 2025.[25] "This is not just an attack on institutions, it's an attack on American values. If we allow our libraries and museums to be defunded and dismantled, if we let history be rewritten to suit political agendas, we will lose more than just funding or access. We will lose the connective tissue within our communities that binds us together. We will lose who we are."

The truth is that demagogues throughout American history have peddled rage and prejudice to justify assaults on our shared ideals. They have exploited public anxiety, whipped up bigotries, and weaponized lies to propel themselves into power and erode fundamental democratic rights. Propagandists in every era have tried, with insidious ingenuity, to manufacture conflict and weaponize lies: that Black people are inherently inferior, that labor organizing is subversion, that homosexuality is a mental illness, that women are too delicate for the responsibilities monopolized by men, that immigrants are vermin invading our country.

* * *

THIS CRISIS is not limited to lies about our past, it is deepened by the relentless attacks on the truth in our present. We now find ourselves in an era when it's increasingly difficult to establish truth amid the welter of information we all consume on a daily basis. Today, disinformation is faster and more powerful; it has been supercharged by deepfakes that distort reality and bots that amplify lies. Algorithms curate our worldviews, trapping us in bubbles that become echo chambers, shielding us from opposing ideas, reinforcing biases, pulling us toward extremism, and numbing us into cynicism and apathy. Social media companies are the tobacco companies of the digital age: designing intentionally addictive products that hook us into heavy use.

As Chris Hayes writes in his book *The Siren's Call*, this new information environment has transformed the way in which we engage in public debate. "The incentives of the attention age create a new model for public debate in which attention is its own end, to be grabbed by any means necessary."[26] He argues that this phenomenon has been both created and perpetuated by tech companies, driven by profit, as they design algorithms that do not try to keep our attention but instead just try to recapture it, over and over again. They have figured out that repeatedly offering us shorter, more sensational content is what keeps us scrolling for as long as possible. He also argues that this has created a world in which the quality of the information we consume is dictated by the method through which we consume it. The consequence of this, according to Hayes, is "that the guy with the loudest megaphone, the most desperate, keening need for attention in perhaps the nation's history, rose to power."[27]

Harkening to demagogues in past eras, Trump uses his megaphone as a tool to spread misinformation, disinformation, and fear. He has captured and recaptured attention on social media and cable news by fabricating and amplifying baseless lies: from the repeatedly disproven claim that he won the 2020 election; to fomenting, denying, and ultimately excusing a violent insurrection; to advancing insane and racist birther conspiracy theories about President Obama and insane and racist accusations of Haitian immigrants eating people's pets in Springfield, Ohio. We are seeing an administration that is disappearing data from the Department of Health and Human Services and the Department of Justice government websites, terminating experts responsible for objective data collection and reporting from the Bureau of Labor Statistics, and firing scientists from the National Institutes of Health and the Centers for Disease Control and Prevention who insist upon grounding their conclusions in scientific evidence.

Add to this that America's adversaries have also figured out how to hack our civic dialogue by infiltrating it with lies. I often descend into the SCIF, or Sensitive Compartmented Information Facility, in the bowels of the Capitol, to receive and read classified briefings about our national security. I am consistently sobered by how much time, money, and energy our adversaries pour into stoking hate, division, and disinformation in our country using digital tools and tricks. The Department of Justice has said publicly that the Russian government has used AI-powered "bot farms" to spread disinformation and stoke division in our country.[28] Our adversaries know they can't beat us tank for tank or aircraft carrier for aircraft carrier. So they try to destabilize what makes our democracy strong: civic trust and a sense of common cause.

These lies do not live in isolation. They destroy trust in our institutions, they weaken our democracy, and they can even be used, as we have seen in our history, as a pretext for violence.

What then is our obligation as Americans? When whistleblowers are hunted and harassed for telling the truth, when prosecutors and law enforcement are fired for doing their jobs, when students are arrested and deported for nonviolent speech, when networks are sued for telling the truth and willingly capitulate to intimidation and journalists and comedians are suspended or silenced for what they write and say, what should we do?

We must look to examples throughout our history. One of the more extraordinary and fearless truth tellers—at a time when truth telling could get you killed—was Ida B. Wells.

In 1892, after writing scathing editorials against the lynching of Black men in Memphis, a white mob stormed Ida B. Wells's office at the *Free Speech and Headlight* newspaper and burned it to the ground. They threatened to kill her if she returned. She was forced to flee the city she called home.[29]

And still, she did not stop.

Even in exile, she investigated lynchings. She named

names, gathered facts, published pamphlets, gave speeches, and built coalitions. Wells endured smear campaigns, violence, and a nationwide press that mocked her, but she refused to stop telling the truth. "The way to right wrongs is to turn the light of truth upon them," she said.[30]

In the face of blatant efforts to hide the truth, erase our history, and advance dangerous lies through relentless repetition, what is needed now is our voices, our commitment to being stewards of the truth. When we remain silent for whatever reason—out of fear or indifference or the cynical belief that what we say won't make a difference—we fail to meet what this moment demands.

Our actions don't have to be large, just persistent. We can be truth tellers in ways that are small but significant, measured yet meaningful.

We all have networks, both online and offline. We can and we must call out misinformation in our conversations with our families and friends, even when it's uncomfortable, and even if it comes from someone on our side of the political divide (and we can be honest and direct without being snarky, condescending, or cruel). We can support the work of journalists at the local and national levels who are dedicated to reporting the truth. We can amplify thought leaders and creators who operate with accuracy and engage with integrity. We can get more involved right where we are—by joining an organization dedicated to issues we care about, attending a public meeting or town hall, showing up at a school board meeting, or joining a local protest and bringing our friends. You can write or call your representatives and let them know that you care about the issues that matter to you—I can tell you that it makes a difference. Most members of Congress are actively tracking the issues, ideas, and concerns that their constituents contact them about. Moreover, when groups of people organize around an issue and coordinate their efforts to send letters and make phone calls to their representatives and senators, it breaks through even more.

* * *

When I entered the Senate in 2013, I thought often of Congressman George Henry White. By then, 135 Black Americans had risen into Congress, even if I was only the ninth to make it to the Senate.[31] And yet, more than a century after White introduced the first antilynching bill, lynching in and of itself was still not a federal crime. Literally hundreds of new crimes have been added to our criminal code, but after more than a century, this horrific injustice was still not federally criminalized.

So, with others, I got to work.

In 2018, for the first time in US history, there were three Black elected senators serving at the same time—

another moment Congressman White could only dream of. I partnered with them—Senator Tim Scott, a Republican from South Carolina, and then Senator Kamala Harris, a Democrat from California—to introduce the Justice for Victims of Lynching Act. Still, the bill stalled. We reintroduced it in the 116th Congress. It was stymied. Then again in the 117th. Through relentless work and negotiation, finally—after more than one hundred years and some two hundred failed attempts—Congress passed a law to make lynching a federal crime.

In his last speech, Congressman White said of the terror of lynching, "This evil peculiar to America, yes, to the United States, must be met somehow, some day."[32] That day came on March 29, 2022, when President Biden signed the Emmett Till Antilynching Act into law, named in memory of the fourteen-year-old Black child who was kidnapped while visiting family in Mississippi and brutally murdered in August 1955. The men who tortured, mutilated, and murdered Emmett Till were never brought to justice. In perhaps one of the most courageous acts of truth telling, Emmett's mother, Mrs. Mamie Till-Mobley, decided that her son's casket would remain open at his funeral for the world to see the horror and vicious hate that took his life. The photographs of Emmett in his casket published by *Jet* magazine shook the nation.

Mrs. Mamie Till-Mobley dedicated the rest of her life

to honoring her son, becoming an activist in the fight for civil rights.

In her book, *Death of Innocence: The Story of the Hate Crime That Changed America*, she wrote, "It is not that I dwell on the past. But the past shapes the way we are in the present and the way we will become what we are destined to become. It is only because I have finally understood the past, accepted it, embraced it, that I can fully live in the moment. And hardly a moment goes by when I don't think about Emmett, and the lessons a son can teach a mother."[33]

5

HUMILITY

The most beautiful thing we can experience is the mysterious. It is the source of all true art and all science. He to whom this emotion is a stranger, who can no longer pause to wonder and stand rapt in awe, is as good as dead: his eyes are closed.

—Albert Einstein, *The World As I See It*

THERE WILL ALWAYS BE A LAST TIME. A FINAL embrace. A last shared laugh. A last kiss. A final goodbye.

For my grandfather and me, our last words felt . . . confusing, at first.

After beating it before, he was once again staring down cancer, and I had flown to see him in Las Vegas. At the end of the visit, I ducked into his bedroom to say goodbye before heading back to the airport.

"How you doing, Granddad?" I asked.

"I'm doing fine," he said, smiling as he picked up a pill

bottle. Quoting one of his favorite movies, he held it up and said, "Say hello to my little friend."

We both laughed.

I was running late for my flight. I dropped my bag, gave him a kiss. "I love you, Granddad," I said.

"I love you," he replied as we hugged. Then, just as I was out the door, he called after me, "I love you. I love your children. I love your grandchildren."

I was thirty-two. I had no children—certainly no grandchildren. But I brushed it off. Maybe it was a joke I didn't get. Maybe he was confused.

I didn't know those would be the last words we ever shared.

* * *

MY MATERNAL grandfather's life was my first history lesson. Born in Jim Crow Louisiana to a thirteen-year-old girl, he stood out among his siblings—lighter skinned, reddish haired. There was a secret that hung over him, unspoken but obvious: His father wasn't his biological father. Once, when he was a boy, his mother took him to see a white doctor, whom he met briefly. Afterward, she told him, without elaboration, "That man is your father." They never spoke of it again. I can only imagine the pain behind that silence.

Why had she gone to visit her child's father? Was she seeking support? Confrontation? Closure?

I don't know all the details of his birth. But I do know he carried the pain of past stigma.

In my grandfather's youth, he endured whispers and outright ridicule. I remember visiting him in Los Angeles when I was in college, and after our usual back-and-forth about my manner of dressing—far too casual for his tastes—I started probing him for more stories about his life and our family history. It was obvious to me that my grandfather must be biracial or have considerable white ancestry. What did he know? I pressed him. The conversation turned from light and easy to suddenly difficult. I could see a long-enduring pain surface in him. He seemed to be preparing himself to say something, and then, almost as a confession, he jarred me with a phrase out of place in my world. "I am illegitimate," he confessed. This shook me, not just because, in my generation, it was a phrase nobody really used anymore, but because I could see the unresolved anguish of it in his pained facial expression. I could see that for him, in his time, the identity of his biological father was not a source of curiosity, it was a curse; it was not a point of interest, it was a source of insults. And perhaps most of all, it was the not knowing. Who was his father? Why hadn't he wanted to be involved in his life? And how, amidst the harsh, even vicious racial segregation, had a man impregnated his mother, then a twelve-year-old girl, and not been held accountable?

And yet, my grandfather was grounded in his faith and his love for his mother and the man who did step forward to raise him. He had a sense of faith about God's plan and purpose—and a humility before all the love that was poured into him by his parents. He taught me that love is stronger than biology, stronger than shame, stronger even than hate.

For my grandfather, love was his purpose. Love big. Love boldly. Love in defiance of every attempt to make you feel small. He believed love could redeem even the most wretched of wrongs and could transform pain into promise, limitations into limitlessness. That belief left him in a near-constant state of humility, instead of the bitterness he might have understandably felt. He lived with an awestruck gratitude for the improbable arc of his life. For decades, he ended every day on his knees in prayers of gratitude.

He went to a historically Black university—the University of Arkansas at Pine Bluff—because his mother insisted he continue his education. She drove him to succeed. There, he met my grandmother: four feet ten inches tall and yet a giant in her own right. He was a physically huge man, but in her, he found his match.

They moved to Detroit. He worked on Ford's Willow Run assembly line during World War II as a member of the United Auto Workers union, building bombers. He became a union organizer. They opened a laundromat, a pool hall, and a gas station. And because I am sure the statute of limitations has now expired, I can confess here that I have been told that my grandfather ran numbers for a while (before the lottery was legit). Then they moved to Los Angeles, where they raised three children—my mother among them. They invested in property, managed their own buildings, made repairs, and rehabbed aging structures, all while working their full-time jobs. They built a family and a future for them that was beyond their dreams.

By the time I was born, they were living what seemed to me a *Jeffersons*-style ascendence: They were moving on up, to a deluxe apartment in the sky, on Wilshire Boulevard in Westwood.

They poured love into their seven grandchildren (of which I was the youngest). They were our directors of fun, and they took us to the best amusement parks near Los Angeles—Knott's Berry Farm, Six Flags Magic Mountain, and, of course, Disneyland. They played with us for hours in the pool and showed intense interest in our lives. I remember my grandfather sitting with rapt attention as if whatever seven-year-old me was telling him was the most important thing he had ever heard. I called him "my pal" as if he was one of my best friends. He made me feel like I was the center of his universe.

When I walked into a room, he would announce me, proclaiming that "Cory the Great!" had entered. He said it so often that I believed it.

But perhaps my most precious memories were of traveling across the country with my grandparents, my brother, and my five cousins in a pea-green motorhome they called *The Green Dream*. Sometimes my grandparents would allow one of our parents to join, but most often, it was just the seven grandchildren and them. Standing at Mount Rushmore, watching sunrises in the Midwest, and playing late-night video games at arcades on the Vegas Strip—we fell in love with America.

I will never forget when our large family, which scarcely ever experienced silence, even in the middle of the night when we were supposed to be sleeping in the cramped camper, stood before the Grand Canyon in hushed awe—from my grandparents through to the youngest, me, words surrendered to the majesty of the landscape.

* * *

NOT LONG after my rushed goodbye and my grandfather's confusing farewell, I was driving down Eighteenth Avenue in Newark when my mother called to tell me the news: Her father, my grandfather, was gone.

Gone was the joy he radiated through my childhood.

The pride in his eyes at every football game he attended, every graduation. The hugs, the humor, the history. Gone.

In my grief, his last words echoed:

"I love you. I love your children. I love your grandchildren."

And suddenly, I understood.

My grandfather was gone, but his love—his fierce, generational love—was still here. He hadn't been confused. He was telling me that he loved me so fully, so fiercely, that his love reached beyond time. He loved generations yet unborn. That was the power of his love. The kind that doesn't stop at death. The kind of love that still resounds in my choices, my voice, my work. The kind of love that will forever ripple forward—through my life, through my future children, and even through strangers who may never know his name . . . but will still feel my grandfather's grace. The kind of love that humbles me still.

* * *

Neil deGrasse Tyson is an astrophysicist. A towering intellect. A PhD. I, on the other hand, am a politician. I have a degree in science too—a bachelor's degree, in political science. With a minor in football (eat your heart out, Neil).

So naturally, between my impressive credentials and the years I spent experimenting with the principles of physics while hitting my head against large bodies of mass on college football fields, I felt very prepared to go toe-to-toe with this brilliant man. To my inner nerd, getting the chance to meet Neil deGrasse Tyson was like visiting Comic-Con and bumping into Obi-Wan Kenobi (and I mean the actual Jedi, not Sir Alec Guinness).

The first time we spoke, I brought up a subject that I thought might rattle him: God. I had remembered hearing that Neil describes himself as agnostic. When answering a question as to whether he believed in an all-powerful, benevolent creator, he said on CBS News *Sunday Morning*, "I have no problems if, as we probe the origins of things, we bump up into the bearded man, if that shows up, we're good to go. OK, not a problem. There's just no evidence of it, and this is why religions are called faiths, because you believe something in the absence of evidence."[1]

I started musing about what happens after you die. I told him about my grandfather's final words to me and how I believed that they were evidence of immortality; I believed that my grandfather's body was gone but that his soul is eternal—he was still with me, watching over me from heaven.

Neil paused and the energy shifted. He met my lighthearted teasing with something deeper. He clearly wasn't rattled, but he wasn't joking around anymore either. He took a breath and said something that surprised me: "OK, Cory. I'm going to get spiritual with you."

He paused. And then he continued, "Cory, when you look up at the sun, you're not seeing it where it is. You're seeing it where it was—eight minutes ago. That's how long it takes light to travel from the sun to us. Five hundred seconds, to be exact."

I nodded, trying to act like I, too, was very attuned to this level of astronomical precision.

"Now you look at the stars at night," he continued. "They're millions of light-years away. Which means you're not seeing them as they are, either—you're seeing them as they were. Some of those stars are already gone—extinct, exploded, dead—but their light is still arriving. Their energy, their warmth, goes on forever."

Then he said, "Cory, we are stardust. The energy we give off in life goes on. Your grandfather is gone in his physical form. But his light, his energy, his warmth—it still travels. It still touches this world and the universe. It clearly still touches you."

And just like that, Neil had out-spiritual-ed me. By inviting me into his sense of awe before the universe, he humbled me.

* * *

Two things fill the mind with ever-increasing wonder and awe, the more often and the more intensely the mind of thought is drawn to them: the starry heavens above me and the moral law within me.

—Immanuel Kant, *Critique of Practical Reason*

I HAVE LEARNED the most about myself when I have been humbled. When I have been reminded of everything I don't know—when an astrophysicist has schooled me on spirituality, when a colleague or staffer has proven me wrong, or when something in my life has turned out to be the exact opposite of what I had predicted, or expected, or in some cases would have hoped.

Those moments, in which I have felt crushed by my own limitations, have always created space. They have expanded my world, asking me not to erase myself or my strongly held beliefs but to step outside of myself.

I have learned that embracing the virtue of humility, whether I choose to be humble or am forcibly humbled, replaces the smallness of my perspective with something bigger and more full of possibility.

I have also learned that as a civic virtue, humility is

what makes the space needed for new ideas, broader strategies, and deeper coalitions. It sharpens your power by opening you up to more people, more perspectives, and more possibilities.

Judge Learned Hand, speaking on "I Am an American Day," May 21, 1944, once captured the essence of this civic virtue: "What then is the spirit of liberty? I cannot define it; I can only tell you my own faith. The spirit of liberty is the spirit which is not too sure that it is right . . . the spirit which seeks to understand the minds of other men and women."[2]

This is the humility that I believe the very survival of our democracy depends on.

The opposite of humility is not pride or even self-assuredness, it is arrogance. It is the belief that there is nothing to gain or learn from listening intently to what others say; arguments are not opportunities to learn, grow, or come to a consensus but are rather monologues where each person waits for the other to stop speaking so they can make their own point.

In our civic life, increasing tribalism has tricked us into thinking that nothing good or even redeemable can come from those in the "other" group. It divides people into camps of the righteous and the irredeemable. It kills curiosity about one another, can crush cooperation, and even, when arrogance embraces cruelty, can turn disagreement into dehumanization.

We are increasingly taught that to doubt our gospel is to be weak, that to question it is to betray, and that listening—not for an opening in which to speak again, but listening with an open heart and open mind—is for losers.

In a deficit of humility in our civic life, this kind of arrogance is celebrated and people marvel at meanness. Bluster is mistaken for strength. And into this vacuum, a certain kind of dangerous leader rises. One who claims he alone can fix it, who tries to sell certainty as safety, who demands loyalty and punishes dissent. One who categorizes constructive critics as "traitors," "the enemy of the people," "un-American," or "fake news" in order to silence and delegitimize them—and even to intimidate others who might join in speaking up.

This is not new. History has shown that when we stop honoring humility, we start elevating a dangerous arrogance, confusing domination for leadership and cruelty for conviction.

A deficit of humility shrinks our imagination, narrows our coalitions. It makes us believe that we already know all we need to know and that anyone who challenges us is an adversary, a threat, an enemy. In the absence of humility, we exchange the difficult work of democracy for the false comfort of obedience and principled leadership for cults of personality.

Humility as a civic virtue, by contrast, invites us to the challenge—to the messy work of our democracy, not to remain apart from it. It doesn't apply a purity test for any potential ally to pass before being welcomed into the fold. It resists the temptation to sit in grievance and gets to work instead—building, uniting, repairing.

There are those who might argue that a moment of crisis for our democracy is not the right time to be discussing the virtue of humility. That humility somehow weakens us in our fight for what we believe in. They would assert that in the toughest fights, in confronting the deepest injustice, there is no tactical advantage found in being humble. But our history shows us that there is strength and strategy in our willingness to engage, listen, learn, and teach; to build broader, more enduring coalitions and grow greater movements. Choosing to embrace humility does not ask us to abandon our anger or surrender our passion, it reminds us that there is a power in engagement that outrage alone cannot access. It is exactly in moments of crisis when the power of humility is needed most.

* * *

IT WAS the afternoon of March 4, 1865, and Abraham Lincoln was surveying the crowd. He had just given his second inaugural address—only 701 words long, it took him just over six minutes to deliver. There was no boasting, no gloating, no triumphant scorn for the vanquished Confederates.

He dared to say plainly that slavery was a principal cause of the war. He framed it as a moral crime with divine consequences: "Yet if God wills that it continue, until all the wealth piled by the bondsman's two hundred and fifty years of unrequited toil shall be sunk, and until every drop of blood drawn with the lash shall be paid by another drawn with the sword, as was said three thousand years ago, so still it must be said: 'The judgments of the Lord are true and righteous altogether.'"[3]

As he spoke honestly, he also summoned the better angels of our nature, speaking of shared humanity and common obligations. He concluded with these immortal words: "With malice toward none, with charity for all, with firmness in the right, as God gives us to see the right, let us strive on to finish the work we are in; to bind up the nation's wounds, to care for him who shall have borne the battle, and for his widow and his orphan—to do all which may achieve and cherish a just, and lasting peace, among ourselves, and with all nations."

It was in this context, after that speech, that Lincoln spotted a Black man—born enslaved—who had been invited to the White House for the postinauguration celebration.

When the man had arrived at Pennsylvania Avenue earlier that day, police officers seized him and his guest, another Black man, and ordered them to step aside, claiming to be acting under orders from the president himself to admit no Black guests.

The man was shocked but steady. He replied that "no such order could have emanated from President Lincoln; and if he knew I was at the door, he would desire my admission."[4]

It was a standoff and a spectacle. Two Black men refusing to be moved, with a growing line of white attendees pressing in from behind, eager to enter the White House. The officers finally ushered the Black men in through the door, but instead of leading them into the reception, they brought them to an exit. At the last minute, another guest recognized the man and came to his aid. It was *Frederick Douglass.*

The officers stood down, and Douglass was finally allowed into the East Room reception.

Just in going to the White House that day, Douglass knew that he would be risking indignity, exclusion, and even assault. But still he went because, as he later wrote, "Now that freedom had become the law of the republic, and colored men were on the battlefield, mingling their blood with that of white men in one common effort to save the country, that it was not too great an assumption for a colored man to offer his congratulations to the President with those of other citizens."[5]

The president of the United States and the Black man who had come to congratulate him both stood out. One towered above the crowd; at six feet four, Lincoln is still the tallest president in American history. The other, Douglass, stood out—because of the color of his skin and because of the power of his presence.

Lincoln saw him and raised his voice for all to hear, unapologetically, proudly, and with a host of intentionality: "Here comes my friend Douglass."

As Douglass approached, Lincoln extended his hand and said, "I am glad to see you. I saw you in the crowd today, listening to my inaugural address. How did you like it?"

Many in the room listened. Some guests were likely annoyed, perhaps even indignant, that a Black man had the president's full attention.

Douglass replied with humility and grace: "Mr. Lincoln, I must not detain you with my poor opinion, when there are thousands waiting to shake hands with you."

Lincoln refused to let him go. "No, no," he insisted. "There is no man in the country whose opinion I value more than yours. I want to know what you think of it."[6]

Over the years, the two had engaged in epic arguments of profound importance. Douglass had confronted Lincoln relentlessly. He had criticized the president's sluggish pace on emancipation, denounced his willingness to consider sending Black Americans, many of whom had been there for generations longer than the nation itself, to Liberia in Africa, and protested the unequal treatment of Black soldiers. When Black soldiers were being denied the right to fight—and once they finally were allowed to fight, when they were being paid less, captured, and killed without consequence—Douglass tirelessly pressed Lincoln, publicly and privately, to act.* From enlistment to equal pay, from prisoner protections to political rights, Douglass never stopped challenging the president, always demanding more.

But from their very first meeting in August of 1863, "even though Douglass found Lincoln's cautious and diplomatic response only partially satisfactory, he came away convinced of the president's sincerity," wrote historian Waldo E. Martin Jr.[7] Lincoln, in turn, knew that Douglass's counsel had shaped his presidency, altering

* Douglass wrote in his *Douglass' Monthly*, "The slaughter of Blacks taken as captives seems to affect him [Lincoln] as little as the slaughter of beeves [cows] for the use of his army."

his strategies and sharpening his own moral compass, and perhaps most importantly, that he had helped win the war.[8] Amidst other feats of leadership, Douglass had helped rally what became nearly 180,000 other Black men to join the Union army and some 19,000 more to join the Navy—heroes who helped preserve the union.[9]

They did not know this would be their last time together.

About a month later, days after Robert E. Lee's surrender, Lincoln would be gone, slain by an assassin's bullet.

But at this moment, history and the president waited for a response.

Abraham Lincoln, as other guests stood and watched, pressed his guest for an answer. He wanted to know what his friend thought of his speech.

And Frederick Douglass, without pretense or performance, looked into the eyes of his friend Abraham Lincoln and offered what would be his final words to the man he had challenged, changed, and come to admire:

"Mr. Lincoln, that was a sacred effort."[10]

* * *

ELEVEN YEARS after Lincoln's assassination, during the collapse of Reconstruction and the rise of racial subjugation, violence, and terror, Douglass stood in Lincoln Park in Washington, DC, for the unveiling of a statue. It was a tribute to Lincoln paid for entirely by formerly enslaved Americans.[11]

The statue depicts a subservient-seeming Black man kneeling before Lincoln. "He did not like the monument," John Stauffer wrote of Douglass in *Giants: The Parallel Lives of Frederick Douglass and Abraham Lincoln*. He saw it as an insult to the role and leadership of Black people in achieving their own liberation. "But he avoided criticizing it, and instead referred to it as a 'highly interesting object' and 'a humble offering,'" Stauffer wrote. "He hoped his speech would offer an antidote to the paternalistic image of a slave kneeling before his white redeemer."[12]

Douglass began his speech that day on a note of pride:

> *I commend the fact to notice; let it be told in every part of the Republic; let men of all parties and opinions hear it; let those who despise us, not less than those who respect us, know that now and here, in the spirit of liberty, loyalty, and gratitude . . . [that] we, the colored people, newly emancipated and rejoicing in our blood-bought freedom, near the close of the first century in the life of this Republic, have now and here unveiled, set apart, and dedicated a monument*

> *of enduring granite and bronze, in every line, feature, and figure of which the men of this generation may read, and those of after-coming generations may read, something of the exalted character and great works of Abraham Lincoln, the first martyr President of the United States.*[13]

But he quickly made clear the purpose of his speech: "Fellow citizens: In what we have said and done today, and in what we may say and do hereafter, we disclaim everything like arrogance and assumption."

He insisted on speaking honestly of Lincoln: "It must be admitted, truth compels me to admit even here in the presence of the monument we have erected to his memory, Abraham Lincoln was not, in the fullest sense of the word, either our man or our model. In his interests, in his associations, in his habits of thought, and in his prejudices, he was a white man. He was preeminently the white man's President, entirely devoted to the welfare of white men."[14]

In the beauty and complexity of the rest of his speech, Douglass found a way to both honor Lincoln and hold him accountable:

> *His great mission was to accomplish two things: first, to save his country from dismemberment and*

> *ruin; and, second, to free his country from the great crime of slavery. To do one or the other, or both, he must have the earnest sympathy and the powerful cooperation of his loyal fellow-countrymen. Without this primary and essential condition to success his efforts must have been vain and utterly fruitless. Had he put the abolition of slavery before the salvation of the Union, he would have inevitably driven from him a powerful class of the American people and rendered resistance to rebellion impossible. Viewed from the genuine abolition ground, Mr. Lincoln seemed tardy, cold, dull, and indifferent; but measuring him by the sentiment of his country, a sentiment he was bound as a statesman to consult, he was swift, zealous, radical, and determined.*[15]

Douglass's speech, like Lincoln's second inaugural, was itself a profound act of civic humility. He honored a man for what he achieved while never excusing what he did not. Exercising humility in our shared civic life does not ask us to surrender the truth, it asks us to have the discipline to see complexity.

In "The Puzzle of Humility and Disparity," a chapter in the *Routledge Handbook of the Philosophy of Humility*, four philosophy professors argue that humility, especially in the context of oppression, is not passivity. It is power.

They point to Douglass's willingness to engage with those he disagreed with, even those who were deeply wrong, as a way of encouraging progress. "Douglass argued that those in the wrong, even those heinously and ridiculously in the wrong, are not beneath our engagement," they write.[16]

Douglass and Lincoln confronted one of the greatest crises in our nation's history not by dismissing each other but by reaching toward each other. By listening. By allowing themselves to be moved—by having humility. They grew in conviction without growing in contempt, and as a result, they discovered common ground, shared meaning, and shared purpose.

The virtue of humility is urgent now, as both a private disposition and a public necessity. We are living through a time of crisis, yes, but more than that, a time of definition and decision. The question we face is not only how to win arguments but how to move a divided, weary, pluralistic nation forward. That cannot happen without humility.

Humility is the foundation of self-examination. It's what allows us to admit that we may not have all the answers, and that there may be truth found even in voices we resist. It demands that we hold ourselves and others accountable. It is also the discipline to listen, especially when it's hard. And it is what gives others the grace to grow.

If we shame people for where they were, instead of creating space for who they might become, then we're simply seeking copies of who we think we are. If we offer no space for people to evolve, to change their minds, then we will never build a movement that transforms society. Shaming may feel righteous in the moment, but it rarely persuades. It hardens hearts. It closes doors. Transformation requires another way.

We cannot cancel everyone who fails a purity test. We cannot exile those who don't align with our every belief, however passionately we hold it. Coalitions that are only composed of the already converted cannot change the country.

If everyone in your coalition agrees with you on everything, your coalition is too small—too small to make big change and too small for what our democracy demands.

And very importantly, when we deny the inevitable complexity of others, we deny it in ourselves. When we deny others the space to grow and evolve, we deny it to ourselves. We are all people in progress. To deny that truth makes you the obstacle to growth, healing, and redemption.

I do not believe the path forward will be forged through arrogant oversimplification or contempt masquerading as clarity. Our democracy cannot be sustained by certainty, it requires humility. Valuing and elevating the virtue of humility is more than a feel-good exercise, it is strategy—it is how coalitions are made, how bridges are built, and how progress, however imperfect, is made real.

What does this look like in practice?

The professors who cite Frederick Douglass in their work on humility and oppression also lift up a modern story: Megan Phelps-Roper, who left behind the antisemitic, antigay Westboro Baptist Church in 2012. They write that "she credits her departure to others outside the Church who engaged her. In her TED Talk, she encourages such engagement: 'My friends on Twitter didn't abandon their beliefs or their principles—only their scorn. They channeled their infinitely justifiable offense and came to me with pointed questions tempered with kindness and humor. . . . They approached me as a human being, and that was more transformative than two full decades of outrage.'"[17] Humility does not mean we let go of truth. It means we hold space for transformation. It asks us not to soften our principles but to deepen our capacity for persuasion and for our own evolution too.

Our founders understood that democracy would require constant revision. That we must be a people more committed to becoming right than merely being right. That humility is the engine of renewal.

And so the work continues: to listen more than we lecture, to build more than we blame. To speak with clarity but not contempt. To recognize our smallness and yet see the grandeur of our shared task, the power of our collective belonging, and the urgency of the unfinished work still to be done.

> *The cosmos is within us. We are made of star-stuff. We are a way for the universe to know itself.*
>
> —Carl Sagan, *Cosmos: A Personal Voyage*

I REACHED OUT to Neil deGrasse Tyson recently to let him know that I was writing about humility and that our conversation years ago had come to mind. I said I wanted to explore how both astrophysics and American history teach us the same lesson: that humility is not a weakness but a necessity. And, since I'm not an astrophysicist, I needed him to confirm that I wasn't completely off base and to get his thoughts about this virtue.

He was enthusiastic. He told me he'd spent a fair amount of time reading the history of science going back several centuries (as one does). What stood out to him, he said, was an observable pattern in many of the greatest scientific minds: They expressed not absolute certainty but profound humility. Even amid their proofs and evidence-based conclusions, they acknowledged that they could be wrong. In their works, they included careful caveats like *this may be right*, or *if this theory fails, it could fail in this way*, or *we need more data to fully understand this.* The boldest thinkers weren't just publishing breakthroughs—they were nodding to their own limitations, their own humanity.

Then Neil told me about Isaac Newton's *Opticks*, his work on the nature of light. In it, Newton did something unusual for his time: He wrote in English, not Latin, as if to invite the common reader into the scientific conversation. At the end, he added a section titled "Queries," where he listed the questions he hadn't yet answered. The man who first calculated gravity left room for wonder and uncertainty. Humility wasn't a sign of weakness but of wisdom. A sign of courage. A willingness to put aside ego in pursuit of truth, to value collective advancement over individual pride.

I reminded him of our talk about the stars and my own beliefs about immortality. I told him that, in this book, I planned to write about the moment when we discussed the death of my grandfather and how his words "we are all stardust" stuck with me—not just to make a point about life after death but about how the vastness of the cosmos should humble us, even as it connects us. I told him I wanted to show that in our smallness, we could discover our expansiveness, we could see that our light, warmth, and even love goes on and on.

We were on a video call. I could see him pause, absorbing what I said. For a moment, he said nothing.

Then he asked, "Can I read you something?"

"Of course," I said.

"It's somewhere in my email here," he said as I watched his eyes dart across the screen in front of him.

When he found what he was looking for, he put on his glasses and began to read:

> Dr. Tyson, I operate a funeral home in western Colorado. We recently had a tragic bus accident that took the life of an 11-year-old girl who was inspired by you. She was cremated with one of your books, and the whole theme of the funeral was astrophysics. The accident gained national coverage, and the family has been through a lot. It would mean the world to them if you could comment on her tribute wall or something similar. I've attached the link. Thank you in advance.

Neil told me that after receiving this message, he looked up everything he could about the girl and found stories about the horrific accident. Her name was Annaliese. She was eleven. At the age of seven, she had already decided she wanted to become an astrophysicist.

Neil posted the following on her memorial page:

> The curiosity of children famously knows no bounds–around the house, the backyard, the neighborhood. Any new place. But when that curiosity includes the universe itself, you're in the presence of someone poised to change the world.
>
> To lose Annaliese at age 11, brimming with so much cosmic ambition, will forever leave me wondering what she might have accomplished as a grown-up kid. Grown-up kids are scientists–and anybody else who retains their childhood curiosity into adulthood. Of course, we will never know the answer to that question.
>
> But we do know the physics of cremation: the energy contents of her body, itself reduced to ash, actually enters Earth's atmosphere. It ultimately escapes to space in the form of infrared energy, radiating in all directions at the speed of light, filling the voids of the cosmos with her presence.
>
> At the moment I write this, Annaliese's energy has extended a half-trillion miles into space–more than 100 times the distance to Pluto.
>
> Though she will live in collective memories for all our lives, in the universe she lives for all eternity.

Respectfully submitted,

Neil deGrasse Tyson

Neil's words honoring a beautiful life tragically cut short illuminated a deeper truth: that in the face of such immensity—of time, space, love, and loss—our humility need not make us feel small.

It can help us recognize that we all are sacred.

6

COMMUNITY

When God had made The Man, he made him out of stuff that sung all the time and glittered all over. Then after some angels got jealous and chopped him into millions of pieces, but still he glittered and hummed. So they beat him down to nothing but sparks, but each little spark had a shine and a song. So they covered each one over with mud. And the lonesomeness in the sparks made them hunt for one another, but the mud is deaf and dumb.

—Zora Neale Hurston,
Their Eyes Were Watching God

I DIDN'T HAVE THE WORDS FOR IT BACK THEN.

I couldn't explain what I was feeling because I didn't fully understand it myself.

In 2004, the language of mental health hadn't entered my world. I didn't know what to call the storm gathering inside me. Looking back now, I know my friends saw it. They commented that I didn't seem like myself. They were worried. But I didn't open up, no matter how hard I was pressed.

What triggered it was a killing.

In 2004, two years after I lost my first race for mayor, my dad was in town for my birthday, and we were out walking through my Newark neighborhood, heading toward the home of some family friends.

Before I could get there, shots rang out. People screamed. Everything sped up and slowed down all at once. It was chaos and commotion. I ran toward the sounds.

A teenager had been shot. I had no training. I pressed my hands to his chest, trying to stop the bleeding. There was so much blood.

The paramedics arrived and loaded him into the ambulance. But I knew he was gone.

His name was Wazn Miller. I had never met him during his life, only during his death.

I don't remember how I got home. I remember standing in the bathroom. I remember looking at myself in the mirror.

I turned on the faucet and began scrubbing the blood from my hands. I kept rubbing, long after the stains were gone. Something within me had ruptured; I felt a darkness I'd never known. Rage. Fear. Shame.

The night after the shooting, I slept fitfully, if at all. I got up early and left my apartment. I had to get out. Just leave. Breathe. Walk.

As I passed through the lobby, I saw Ms. Virginia Jones, our tenant leader in Brick Towers, where I lived, and a bedrock of our community.

Ms. Jones had moved into Brick Towers—two sixteen-story low-income buildings connected by a courtyard—in 1970 as one of the first residents when the buildings opened. She was elected tenant president then and remained so through the entire life of the buildings.

Over the course of decades, Ms. Jones saw her community overrun by powerful, generational forces—from redlining and disinvestment to surrounding towns pushing their environmental hazards out of their communities and into Newark.

She saw how her community was undermined and attacked by government corruption, greed, and bigotry. She understood the incalculable damage of a drug war that arrested thousands of Newark kids for the same nonviolent crimes that so many of my peers in college and grad school committed just as frequently while escaping the life-altering damage that comes with arrest records or drug convictions and incarceration.

Ms. Jones also saw what disparities in access to healthcare did to the bodies and mental health of her neighbors.

She saw how underinvestment in Newark's schools constricted the preparation and opportunities of her kids. And she saw violence.

In 1980, her own son, a member of the armed forces, was murdered at Brick Towers. After the shooting, she was pulled from her apartment in one of the buildings into the lobby of the other. She got there in time to see her son bleeding out onto the floor.[1]

And yet Ms. Virginia Jones never left those buildings or abandoned her role as their leader. I often wondered why. Why would she stay in the place where her greatest life trauma occurred? She hadn't run or retreated, she only fought harder for our community—she became more of an activist for the children of Brick Towers and beyond. She went on to help lead an alliance of tenant associations throughout the city. That thought clung to me as I walked into the courtyard. Then I saw her.

She was standing at the front entrance to the complex, her back to me. The small, elderly sentinel of Brick Towers was standing at her post.

I stopped. Fifty feet away. Staring.

She turned. She saw me. She said nothing.

She did what I needed her to do, she just opened her arms.

I ran to her. I'm six foot three, and she barely reached

my chest, but she felt like a giant, holding me completely.

Through her embrace—her love—she reminded me that I wasn't alone. There was no shame in drowning. There was no easy way out. But there was a way through.

* * *

WE ARE facing a crisis in this country. A crisis of loneliness. A crisis of separation, isolation, and disconnection. A crisis of faith in one another.

This is a crisis of community.

The sources of strength that deepened our communal bonds, the places where people gathered, connected, and saw one another—the main street hardware store, the block party, the house of worship, the local newspaper that told our community stories—have been drained and many replaced by home delivery, home entertainment, and technologies that promise connection but often deliver only distance and division.

A quarter century ago, Robert Putnam issued a warning in *Bowling Alone*: "For the first two-thirds of the twentieth century a powerful tide bore Americans into ever deeper engagement in the life of their communities, but a few decades ago—silently, without warning—that tide reversed and we were overtaken by a treacherous rip current. Without at first noticing, we have been pulled apart from one another and from our communities over the last third of the century."[2]

That tide has only receded further. As former Surgeon General Vivek Murthy wrote in his 2023 advisory titled *Our Epidemic of Loneliness and Isolation*, about half of adults in America report experiencing loneliness.[3]

Without true community, we don't just lose touch with others—we lose ourselves. Much of our sense of belonging, identity, and meaning is forged in the presence of others. And when crisis strikes—personal or collective—it is community that grounds us. Like trees in a forest, rooted together, we withstand storms better when we are not alone.

Loneliness, neuroscientist John Cacioppo and his coauthor, William Patrick, observed, "disrupts the regulation of key cellular processes deep within the body."[4] This disruption, according to Surgeon General Murthy's report, "is associated with a greater risk of cardiovascular disease, dementia, stroke, depression, anxiety, and premature death. The mortality impact of being socially disconnected is similar to that caused by smoking up to 15 cigarettes a day."[5] This is not merely philosophy. It is biology. We evolved over millennia in tight-knit, interdependent communities. Human beings were never meant to go it alone. Our wiring is for connection. In their book, *Loneliness: Human Nature and the Need for Social Connection,* Cacioppo and Patrick observed that loneliness has an evolutionary function—it is the human body's reminder to itself that it needs community to survive, functioning in the same way that hunger and thirst are the body's alarm systems that a critical physical need is not being met. As a result, they noted, "when we feel isolated, we also feel embattled"—isolation activates a feeling of danger in our bodies.[6] When this feeling "settles in," it makes us hypervigilant to the threat of rejection, creating a self-reinforcing cycle that breeds distrust.[7] This negative feedback loop means that people who feel lonely are more likely to feel like they are under constant attack. They are also more likely to feel like they, in a sense, will always be lonely. "When we feel lonely, we are painfully aware that our social needs are not being met; at the same time, we have a greater tendency to see ourselves as having little control over our ability to fulfill those needs," Cacioppo and Patrick wrote, adding that this "makes us even more likely to behave in self-protective ways that spin the feedback loop further and faster toward even more isolation."[8] This deepens our self-protective instincts, feeding the very isolation we long to escape.

That hunger for safety and belonging, when not met in healthy ways, can be exploited in toxic ones. "The tribalist is seeking connection," *New York Times* columnist David Brooks writes, "but isolates himself ever more bitterly within his own resentments and distrust. Tribalism is the dark twin of community."[9]

Disconnected from authentic community, we turn to belonging built on bitterness.

Psychotherapist Esther Perel points to another cruel irony: "Modern loneliness masks as hyper-connectivity. It's not about being physically alone, but about being misunderstood, unseen, rejected, ostracized."[10]

Social media promises us connection but often leaves us both feeling lonely and feeling crazy for feeling lonely. It sorts us into tribal identities, reduces us to incomplete digital personas, and profits from igniting our outrage and our fear. It replaces fellowship with false fights. The result has been a form of spiritual violence—wounding our emotional well-being, eroding our social fabric, and further isolating us from each other. What begins as isolation can harden into rage. What starts as a yearning for belonging can be hijacked by counterfeit communities that peddle in grievance and even extremism.

What makes this crisis all the more dangerous for our democracy is that it is constantly eroding our sense of common cause. The idea of the common good is vanishing as corporations, networks, and social media platforms constantly tell us how much we should be outraged by each other, how much we should hate one another, and how much we should continue to widen the perceived schism between us and them.

Further under assault is our understanding that our well-being is tied to that of our neighbors—that their joy, struggle, safety, and flourishing are linked to ours. More and more, we see one another not as fellow countrymen and countrywomen, sharing destiny with collective aspirations and a larger common good, but as detriments to each other, as daily annoyances and even as existential threats.

This is cancerous to a democracy. In *How Democracies Die*, Steve Levitsky and Daniel Ziblatt write, "If one thing is clear from studying breakdowns throughout history, it's that extreme polarization can kill democracies."[11]

We can't forget where our true strength comes from. Yes, individual striving matters—ambition, grit, discipline, and personal excellence. But we are not merely individual actors. We rise or fall together. Teams multiply potential. Children raised in a community of care—a neighborhood that nurtures and a culture that connects—don't just survive. They thrive. But when humans are isolated, alone, and disconnected, it can not only lead to individual suffering but can have dangerous effects on neighborhoods, cities, and entire nations.

My own experiences have made me particularly worried about the corrosive power of loneliness and how it can become especially explosive in men. Vivek Murthy notes that men and women experience loneliness at roughly equal rates—but men often express it in very different, and often destructive, ways. "Loneliness can masquerade as lots of different things. In men, anger and short-temperedness is a common way that loneliness manifests," he said in a conversation with Arthur Brooks.[12] That anger, Murthy writes in his powerful book *Together,* is "one of the few emotions a man can express and still feel masculine."[13]

Short fuses, when lit, can be highly combustible.

* * *

IN THE months after the shooting, I was enveloped by a despair I could not shake or describe to others. Even getting out of bed was a battle; getting dressed and leaving the apartment felt like it took all my energy. Moving through my day felt like trying to walk underwater.

And above all, I felt powerless. Everywhere I looked, there was an accommodation of injustice—deep, structural, and ignored. Violence, random and routine. Poverty that persisted no matter how hard people worked. Slumlords profiting from human suffering. Children poisoned by lead. Families bankrupted by ER visits, after being denied the care that would have prevented the emergency in the first place. A justice system where kids were caged for the same mistakes my college peers at Stanford made without consequence. Addiction met not with treatment but with incarceration. A community rich in promise but robbed, exploited, forgotten.

I was failing. I had asked thousands of people to pour their hopes into my dream of making a difference. But I had lost the mayor's race. I was no longer on the city council, a position of power to object, expose, and challenge the wrongs going on in the city. I felt like a ghost, moving through my city but feeling unable to touch or make much of an impact on what mattered. And I felt guilty and embarrassed for even feeling this way, as I imagined the unbearable pain that Wazn's family and friends, who knew and loved him, were feeling—and so many others with justifiable reasons for grief, anguish, or rage.

I wish I could go back in time and speak to my younger self the way I now try to show up for friends who are struggling: *It's OK. It's OK to struggle. It's OK to feel overwhelmed, to feel like you can't figure it all out on your own. And most importantly, it's OK to ask for help—to lean on others, to go to therapy.* But I didn't do any of those things, I didn't talk to people around me. I carried it all alone.

Frustratingly, even today, over twenty years later, too many still don't reach out for professional help either because of stigma or obstacles to care. I am encouraged by more people speaking to this stigma, including a number of prominent men who are comfortable speaking openly about their struggles with mental health—we need to see more of this.

However, therapy is too expensive, and for many it can be extremely difficult to find a therapist who is culturally competent. Our mental health treatment system is still grossly inadequate to meet the demands of our nation, and so many suffer unnecessarily.

Our schools are ill-equipped to deal with the growing youth mental health crisis.[14] With the lack of mental health professionals in our schools, our teachers are more and more asked to play roles that they aren't trained for and that impinge upon their classroom instruction. It is also ridiculous that we have asked our nation's police officers to grapple with our collective failures to create a mental health treatment system that serves our communities. Our nation's prisons and jails have become our biggest mental health treatment facilities.[15] Study after study has demonstrated that better access to community-based mental health treatment is far more effective, can be dramatically less expensive, and is profoundly more humane.[16] The opioid epidemic is now the deadliest drug crisis in our country's history,[17] and while there are many reasons for this, the medical community has pointed to untreated mental health issues as a major risk factor for opioid abuse.[18]

Building spaces of connection, understanding, and care is not a cure-all for the challenges we face, but it is where healing and resilience can begin.

* * *

FIFTEEN MONTHS after the shooting, on a summer afternoon, I was invited to a youth basketball tournament at Pennington Court, a sprawling public housing complex in the East Ward of Newark. I was still trying to fill the dark hole left behind, rebuilding emotionally and spiritually, and had thrown myself into preparing for another mayoral run, hoping the clarity of an external mission might calm the ache I still carried.

I was one of the event's sponsors. I had friends there. I had knocked on every door in that community—more than once. I'd been a regular at tenant meetings and had helped residents with everything from legal issues to job opportunities. Pennington Court felt like home. In fact, it was one of the areas we'd won in my first, unsuccessful run for mayor.

But when I arrived for the tournament, members of Mayor Sharpe James's security detail approached me.

James, who had defeated me in the previous election, was in his fourth term as mayor.

"You have to leave," they said. I was stunned. This was a public event. There was no reason for me to be removed—except that the mayor was on his way and didn't want me there. They asked me to leave three times. Three times, I refused. Finally, one of them said, "If you don't leave, we may have to arrest you."

That set me off. Since I first ran against him for mayor in 2001, James had tried to harass and intimidate me—he sought not just to defeat me in elections but to leave me defeated in the broadest sense of the word. I'd been subjected to years of police harassment—tickets on my car when parked legally, tapped phones, and being followed, surveilled, and bullied.[19]

And now, finally, I snapped.

"Go ahead," I said. "Arrest me. Let's see what happens."

They backed off. But the tension didn't.

The mayor arrived in full spectacle—cars, security, handshakes, waving crowds. Then he saw me.

He exploded. "What is he doing here?" he yelled. "He doesn't belong here. He's a loser from the Central Ward."

Something broke loose inside of me. I yelled back. Loud. Petty. Ugly.

He responded. He tore into me. And soon we were off. We squared up to each other. Supporters lined up behind and around us. The basketball games stopped. Crowds gathered. Reporters arrived.

The hot summer blacktop blistered with rage. We closed in on each other until we stood face-to-face, shouting. I could feel the heat of his breath, the spray of spittle from his mouth.

The mayor of the city taunted me, threatening to knock me out. This only fanned the flame of my anger. "You want to hit me? Come on, hit me," I shouted back at a man my father's age.

Two grown men, shouting like kids, posturing like boxers. The crowd around us was stunned, outraged, entertained.

Then an officer on the mayor's security team lost it. Enraged, he stepped between us—nose to nose with me now. The shouting escalated. Supporters began shoving. Something primal kicked in. Rational thought evaporated. We were a group of large men, puffed up, posturing, digging in, daring one another.

The officer in front of me was clearly losing control. His hand hovered near his holstered weapon. His face flushed red with fury. Others around him sensed it too—they rushed in, grabbing and restraining him as he thrashed against them.

And what did I do? I poured gasoline on his fire.

"Let him go!" I shouted. "Come on!" I pounded my chest with my fist. "Bring it!" I roared, daring him forward, overflowing with bravado and recklessness.

No one was watching the kids anymore. The kids were watching us.

People spilled out of buildings, drawn by the noise. A larger crowd gathered than the game had attracted. It was a circus. And we were the clowns.

The next day, *The Star-Ledger* ran a photo of the confrontation, showing me and the mayor's security detail staring each other down. I'll never forget that article:

> The Battle of the Bricks basketball tournament was intended to provide youth from different Newark Housing Authority complexes with a positive outlet for dealing with each other. Instead, the youth watched yesterday as a political clash erupted between Mayor Sharpe James and mayoral candidate Cory Booker at the Pennington Court housing projects. James called Booker's associates a "goon squad" and "political whores." . . . Moore went after Oscar James Jr. and Booker, but Police Chief Irving Bradley blocked the hard-charging officer, who appeared to reach for his weapon. Bradley said the officer

> was not reaching for his weapon, but trying to protect the mayor.[20]

The New York Times described it this way: "Shouting epithets and pushing, a mass of more than 20 people moved from the edge of one basketball court to the other. At one point, one of the mayor's more muscular security guards, had to be restrained by several people as Mr. Booker said, 'Come on, come on,' waving his hands toward his chest."[21]

Residents were furious, disappointed, and hurt by our actions. Rightly so.

It didn't take long for me to feel sick with shame. And then fear. Because far scarier than a standoff with the mayor and his security team was having to face Ms. Virginia Jones.

Ms. Jones had an unrivaled communications network, one that could put a cable company out of business. She did not need to pick up the phone to get in touch with someone in Brick Towers. When she put the word out, her messages carried. So it wasn't long after the fight when I got the first "Ms. Jones is looking for you" while walking through the courtyard between our buildings. Soon there were several more "You need to see Ms. Jones" and a "Ms. Jones wants to talk to you." Folks were urgent, almost demanding, and they seemed to know . . . I was in trouble.

I knew what I had to do. I went to her apartment.

Ms. Jones and her right hand, Ms. Jean Wright, two of the mighty matriarchs of our community, didn't hold back.

Ms. Jones went in on me, saying something like, "Who was that at Pennington Court? I know that wasn't Cory Booker! You are supposed to be our hope. You swinging your ego around like a wrecking ball—tearing down what we're trying to build."

She finally asked, "You lost yourself? You want me to knock some sense back into you? God don't like ugly. You need some prayer, you need to ask for some forgiveness."

Ms. Jean Wright stood beside her, arms crossed, nodding and punctuating her points with an occasional "Mmm-hmm" and "That's right."

Then Ms. Jones leaned in even harder.

"You are different," she snapped. "You hear me? You are different! Do you remember that? Don't you *ever* betray that."

Her words hurt, but they reminded me of who I was—and who I wanted to be. She didn't shame me into exile. She loved me back into alignment. She called me out *and* called me home.

That's what community does.

* * *

We face a crisis of "us vs. them," of in-group and out-group thinking. A healthy community doesn't cancel for disagreement, it doesn't cast out or ostracize when someone fails, falters, or falls—or even when someone dissents. A community refuses the easy comfort of purity. It knows that belonging isn't earned by perfection but is ultimately sustained by grace. Community heals division and individuals not by drawing harder lines of exclusivity but by building stronger bridges of connection.

I am grateful and fortunate that I had Virginia Jones and Jean Wright to intervene on that occasion and on so many more. I have learned that when institutions fail to meet people's emotional and existential needs, when government, faith communities, schools, or neighborhoods stop offering each other—our families, our children—real spaces for meaning and belonging, others can step in.

And too often, they will offer a dark, shadow version of what we've failed to provide.

I believe that men are particularly vulnerable to this counterfeit version of connection: one that doesn't heal but hardens. One that doesn't create solidarity but stokes suspicion.

As Scott Galloway writes, "Boys also face unique threats which have been getting more ominous in recent years—and they are ill prepared for these challenges by a culture that conflates masculinity with toxicity and aggression with strength. Men are twice as likely to overdose, three and a half times more likely to commit suicide and are more than nine times more likely to be incarcerated."[22]

For many men—historically and still today—identity and social standing are rooted in being a provider: having a good job, owning a home, supporting a family, building a secure life. But for too many, these basic pillars are slipping out of reach.

Facing these crises—and a culture that still too often makes men feel weak for expressing emotion or a need for connection—we see how online spaces become the only easily accessible places where men feel seen and find community. In these spaces, charlatans and cynical politicians often step in to tell men the lie that their genuine struggles and frustrations are the fault of women, of immigrants, of anyone else they can scapegoat.

This should be a wake-up call for all of us.

We ignore this crisis at our peril, not only for the sake of men, but for the health, strength, and safety of our entire society. We need to reclaim and rebuild the spaces where all of us—boys and men included—are allowed to feel, to struggle, to seek help, and to belong. We need communities rooted in care, in accountability, and in shared purpose.

We need more spaces where men can show up as their full selves, where boys, as they are taught that misogyny and sexism are wrong, are also taught that they are worthy and that *their masculinity is not toxic* but valued and needed. Where they're taught that there's nothing masculine about punching down—about using their strength to target those who are struggling or cast out for being different. Real strength protects vulnerable people. It doesn't prey on them. And the measure of a man—and of our humanity—is found in whether we look out for the least among us, for those who've been cast aside and need someone strong to have their back.

We need more spaces where men and boys find connection based on their common aspirations, not their grievances, and where they are empowered to be part of solutions rather than simply be told again and again that they are the problem.

Throughout my life, I've seen the power of the kinds of spaces that nurture belonging and community and celebrate masculinity. I've seen how they can heal, empower, and anchor a person in something deeper than ambition or survival. I found brotherhood through sports, bonds forged on courts and fields that endure decades later. Beyond my father, my uncles, my older brothers, and the men of my church, I found healthy models of masculinity and connection in sports—in particular, in football. My teammates and I didn't just sweat and struggle together. In that shared striving, we created a community not just of grit and glory but of vulnerability, empathy, and care. I feel blessed that my crew of high school football teammates are still connected, still friends, and still make time to get together. We are all over the political spectrum, racially and religiously diverse, but we share a bond deeper than the lines that too often divide our nation.

Just a year after the intervention of Virginia Jones and Jean Wright, and without a doubt because of that intervention, I stayed in community, grew greater coalitions, and then did go on to win at the ballot box. And as mayor, I tried to replicate the community building they had modeled for me.

Too many young people in crisis in our city, and in other communities across the country, were being swept into the criminal justice system, where their lives unraveled further and faster, trapping individuals and creating intergenerational cycles of unaddressed trauma.

If there's anything I heard from the community, it's that gangs were serving a purpose—they had become a dangerous substitute for missing mentorship, meaning, and fellowship. So we worked to create constructive spaces in Newark where men could show up for each other, be safe, and be fully seen.

One of the many ways we worked to build constructive community was an initiative that began with a simple question: *Do you want to be a great dad?*

We asked that question to men returning home from incarceration. Many were overcome with emotion at the question—some with pride, some with pain, some with a combination of both. Many had never been asked anything like it before. Most stepped up with a fierce, affirmative yes.

From that question, we built something beautiful: a male fraternity called Delta Alpha Delta Sigma—DADS.[23]

We invited groups of men to join this brotherhood, organized around their deepest *why*—why they were striving to rebuild, to heal, to thrive, to be a great father. The fraternity offered parenting classes, job readiness training, counseling for mental health and addiction, dental and medical services, and more. But just as importantly, it offered *each other*. A support system. A sacred circle. A new kind of family.

Together, they became a community not just for themselves but for their children, their partners, and their neighborhoods. They attended events as fathers with their children. In their fraternity meetings, they often had emotional conversations—about fear, hope, grief, and growth. They traded practical advice: how to get through the hard days, how to show up strong, how to stay on the path. They broke bread together. They held each other accountable.

For years, the fraternity was an extraordinary success. Not only did we see a low recidivism among the men who participated, but we witnessed something even more powerful: transformation. These men weren't just staying out of prison. They were becoming pillars—fathers, mentors, providers, leaders. They were breaking cycles of trauma and disconnection. They were building something that could last. Moreover, everyone involved, including the coaches, counselors, and doctors, saw themselves improving and benefiting as part of the community.

The fraternity graduations were unforgettable. Men walking across the stage—some with young children in their arms—radiating strength, pride, and joy. The room would erupt with cheers and applause from a full house: kids, mothers, family members, and their fraternal brothers.

> *Community is . . . a bunch of people looking after each other. A bunch of people seeing each other—and seeing each other deeply. Taking the time to really enter into a relationship with one another, to depend on one another, to buttress each other's stories, and to buttress each other's behavior . . . the end result of all this is a sort of joyfulness. You can be happy alone—you win a game, you get a promotion, you feel big about yourself. Happiness is the expansion of self. But joy is the merger of self. It's what happens when you forget where you end and something else begins—when you really are seeing deeply into each other.*
>
> —David Brooks, "Finding the Road to Character"

THAT KIND of joy is at the heart of community. We can often feel the potential of this, the spirit of this, at religious services, concerts, and even sporting events—a powerful, joyous, and even transcendent spirit of connection to those around us that belies any of the grievances peddled by powerful people who benefit from our division.

I have also seen this spirit when joy leaves us—after natural disasters, when some awful event literally shakes us or washes away so much that we see the best of humanity, the best of human generosity, in what is left. We see neighbor helping neighbor, people pulling together with the realization that despite our losses and our brokenness, we are defiantly still strong. After Superstorm Sandy, we were "Jersey Strong"—amidst pain, loss, and grief, we found community anew, and in that healing, hope, and heart, we found each other.

Community is the idea that we are responsible for one another. That we belong to one another. That our destinies are intertwined.

I believe that policy-making has an essential role to play in building and repairing community. In the Senate, I fight for policies like expanding the child tax credit, securing paid family leave, and making high-quality childcare and early childhood education affordable and universal. But this crisis isn't only a matter of public policy. It's deeper than law or legislation. Confronting the erosion of community also demands something personal. Definitionally, it calls each of us into the work.

So I don't believe that we will build community with some grand, national project announced from a podium. Because healing doesn't begin there. Experts from Dr. Murthy to Dr. Cacioppo agree: To confront the crisis of loneliness, we must start right where we are. "The key is to ease your way into it . . . to be able to test other ways of behaving without that feeling of danger, you need a safe place to experiment, and you need to start small," Cacioppo and Patrick suggest.[24] Dr. Murthy recommends, "Dedicate at least fifteen minutes each day to connecting with those you most care about."[25]

Creating community begins with how we see each other, how we treat those closest to us. Do we notice the people around us? Do we reach out to neighbors in times of need? Are we present with others? Do we extend grace and empathy?

I marveled for years at the fact that Virginia Jones never left the neighborhood where her son was murdered. I saw her as heroic, and she is. But now I also understand something else. Ms. Jones stayed in the place where her deepest trauma had occurred because she knew that strength doesn't come from solitude or in exile, it rises in connection, in rootedness, in community.

7

CREATIVITY

The universe is full of magic things patiently waiting for our wits to grow sharper.

—Eden Phillpotts, *A Shadow Passes*

THE MAYOR OF NEWARK, NEW JERSEY WANTS TO set up a citywide program to improve residents' health," said Conan O'Brien, the tall, tousled titan of *The Tonight Show*. I sat up. I had grown up watching this show—that famous curtain, that flood of light, as that host stepped on to the screen and into America's living rooms, bringing a spark of joy. The light was coming our way . . . finally. A national spotlight on something positive from our city. I put down my two best friends, Ben and Jerry, and I reached for my phone to call my mom. We were on TV!

It was 2009. I had returned home after another marathon day as mayor of Newark. Our city was fighting forward. We were stubbornly rising through the wreckage of a global recession, a national housing crisis, and decades of disinvestment and damaging policies like redlining and failed urban renewal projects that punished cities like ours.

My seven-plus years as mayor of Newark were some of the hardest and most rewarding days of my life. Newark believed in Newark, even when the rest of the country seemed not to. We were battling an intolerably high poverty rate, a severe housing shortage, and a stubbornly high crime rate. And just as we were beginning to fight back, the global recession hit. The housing bubble burst, the national economy buckled, and unemployment in the nation, as well as Newark, surged. But despite the considerable challenges facing us, we didn't stop. We fought to turn the tide—and slowly, we had begun to see results. Crime dropped. Affordable housing projects broke new ground, defying national trends. We were laying the foundation for what would become Newark's largest business and economic development boom in over half a century. But none of it came easy. Making progress felt like running through waist-deep water—slow, exhausting, but steady. Each day brought a new push forward: building parks and schools, attracting investment, designing new strategies to meet our residents' needs. Momentum was building. Change was coming.

Yet, the reputation that tenaciously clung to the city—one of crime, corruption, decline—made it difficult to convince people to invest in Newark, visit Newark, join in the cause of Newark. The national media didn't help. Even though we were making notable strides in public safety, the stories they told about Newark continued to emphasize poverty and crime. If it bleeds, it leads. Still, we poured enthusiasm into our work every day, launching new initiatives and finding creative ways to help residents, strategies that eventually began to get some attention. One innovation I was particularly proud of was the plan we devised to reduce prescription drug costs for many residents at local pharmacies.

And now, on national TV, on a historic and beloved American program, Conan O'Brien continued his monologue: "The mayor of Newark, New Jersey wants to set up a citywide program to improve residents' health. . . . The healthcare program would consist of a bus ticket out of Newark." Cue record scratch! Oof.

I didn't call my mom. I reached instead for Ben & Jerry. Sadly, even a premium swirl of peanut butter and pretzels couldn't cool my rising temperature as the talk show tyrant punched down on our city. But before I hit the rock-bottom, numbing embrace of a food coma, I realized Conan had just handed me an opportunity. Traditional media may have taken a cheap shot at us, but I had something mayors in America didn't have just a few years before—Twitter.

This was the dawn of social media, when Twitter still had that new-hope-for-democracy glow. This was before the bots and the bile, before a billionaire bought the platform and changed its name. People still believed it could be a place for supercharging democracy and expanding connection and engagement on things that mattered.

And so I started tweeting with residents. "See a pothole? Tweet me." "Streetlight out? Tweet me." I answered constituents directly and sometimes in real time, turning Twitter into a kind of virtual town hall. Soon, people were tweeting me about stray dogs, traffic accidents, snowed-in streets—and I responded, often around the clock. It helped hold us accountable; I was crowdsourcing government improvement. And Newark's residents found it empowering too. Instead of just driving by something they saw wrong, people took action. Soon we were finding out about issues almost instantaneously and could address them much more quickly, which only encouraged more people to speak up and help us identify more issues. It was a virtuous cycle.

This became a small part of our larger effort to change Newark's narrative. As my Twitter following grew, hundreds of thousands of people who likely would have never before paid attention to Newark began to witness our work. Now I'd be able to leverage that awareness. Conan O'Brien had given me the perfect opportunity to use social media to punch up and fight back on behalf of Newark. So we made a video. I played up the outrage, mock solemnity, and deadpan seriousness. "According to the powers invested in me by the people of the city of Newark," I declared, "I am officially putting you on the Newark, New Jersey, airport no-fly-list. Try JFK, buddy."

The video went viral.

Phone lines at city hall lit up. I started receiving calls from First Amendment absolutists who were earnestly concerned that we had violated Conan's civil liberties in banning him from the airport. The story got so big that the TSA even felt the need to post an official statement clarifying that no, American mayors cannot actually ban comedians from airports. Satellite trucks rolled up around Newark City Hall to cover the story—not a tale of crime or corruption, but a fake feud over a late-night joke. I played it up, and interview requests came pouring in. All of a sudden, I had a bigger platform to defend Newark, celebrate our progress, and make the case for our city.

And then to my delight, Conan responded. On air.

He played my video to his millions of viewers and announced—by the power vested in him by his studio audience—that I was officially banned from the Burbank airport.

Burbank? Not a big deal. I use LAX.

But it was the principle. So I became even more fake furious. It was on.

I fired back. This time, I banned him from the entire state of New Jersey. (I also would have banned him from listening to two patron saints of New Jersey, Springsteen and Bon Jovi, but I worried about violating the Eighth Amendment, which prohibits cruel and unusual punishment.)

Our feud made national headlines. I made the rounds from daytime chat shows to talk show legends like Larry King, roasting Conan and—more importantly—evangelizing Newark: our incredible transit access, our universities, our culture, our comeback.

And then an unimaginable diplomatic intervention came: Secretary of State Hillary Clinton—yes, the actual secretary of state—filmed a video for *The Tonight Show* urging Conan and me to end our feud. She told us that "the time has come to make peace . . . end this silly feud and you can go back to what you both do best. For Mayor Booker, that means leading Newark toward a new era of growth and prosperity. For Conan, that means dancing around the stage and making lame jokes about my pantsuits. Thank you. And, Conan, please don't bother me again."

In years past, a mayor whose city was insulted could have written an angry letter to the network that might be read weeks later by an intern's intern. Or they could have called a press conference to blast the late-night host, but they would have been lucky to get channel 148 (the National Norwegian Network) to show up and pay attention. But now the secretary of state was intervening and helping to defend the honor and promise of our community.

And before long, the kid who grew up watching Johnny Carson's curtain open found himself standing behind it. My name was called. I walked out on *The Tonight Show* stage, before a national audience, crossed over to the Lanky Leprechaun of Late Night Lies, and we shook hands as a first step in burying the hatchet. Conan said many people had made fun of Newark before and asked why I had gone after him with an airport ban. I basically replied that when you're a lion looking at a herd, you go after the weakest gazelle.

We laughed. We sparred. And then Conan did something extraordinary: He apologized to Newark. And he and NBC donated $100,000 to charitable causes in Newark. I lifted the ban. Conan was again welcome to visit New Jersey.*

The Conan kerfuffle gifted us something lasting. More calls returned. More meetings taken. More interest from

* It's been fifteen years, and I still don't know if he has come to Jersey yet. Come on, Conan, meet me at a Jersey diner for some disco fries.

developers, investors, foundations, and philanthropists. Our viral fake battle helped advance the cause of Newark, bringing measurable resources to our city. It let the whole country see our grit, our humor, our progress, and our promise, and it made more people want to be a part of our success story. It made them question their misconceptions and indifference toward Newark and sparked attention, curiosity, engagement, and ultimately more partnerships.

Our real fight wasn't with Conan, of course—it was with the misperceptions, the stereotypes, and the indifference that too many Americans held about Newark and many other urban places.

To many people, Newark wasn't a real place, it was a punch line. A city defined not by its people or potential but by its problems. It was "over there"—that place you drive past or through as quickly as you can. The place that's someone else's responsibility and burden. There are many places in America where people don't see the fullness of a community or don't see beyond caricatures that undercut truth and potential.

Indifference is the enemy of community. It allows a dangerous delusion to take root: that what happens to someone else has no effect on us, that we are isolated individuals rather than part of an interconnected whole. And as Elie Wiesel said, "Indifference is never creative."[1] It deadens our moral imagination—our ability to see others as a vital part of ourselves—and weakens our capacity to creatively respond when others face injustice.

Persistent injustice thrives on indifference. To combat indifference, you don't just throw more facts, policy proposals, or righteous indignation at people. To inspire, to raise awareness or persuade people to activism, you must be more creative.

* * *

UNDESIRABLE, UNSEXED, *dangerous*, *crazy*, and *pathological* were the words used to describe the first group of people in American history to protest in front of the White House.[2]

Twelve women had gathered at the gates on January 10, 1917, urging President Woodrow Wilson to support an amendment granting women the federal right to vote.

They did not chant or shout but instead stood silently. As suffragist and author Doris Stevens later recounted in her extraordinary book, *Jailed for Freedom*, "Here were we, citizens without power and recognition, with the only weapons to which a powerless class which does not take up arms can resort . . . our simple, peaceful, almost quaint device—a banner."[3] They became known as the Silent Sentinels.

Using their banners and a unique and extraordinary strategy, they appealed directly to President Woodrow Wilson, pointing out the hypocrisy in his soaring rhetoric about fighting for democracy abroad during World War I while failing to make its promise real at home.

On the first day of the protest, their banner read, "Mr. President! How long must women wait for liberty?"[4]

On a day that Russian diplomats visited the White House, their banner read, in part, "We the Women of America tell you that America is not a democracy. Twenty million American women are denied the right to vote. President Wilson is the chief opponent of their national enfranchisement. Help us make this nation really free. Tell our Government it must liberate its people before it can claim Free Russia as an ally."[5]

On the Fourth of July, their banner simply read, "Governments derive their just powers from the consent of the governed."[6]

Months after America entered into World War I, their banner asked, "Kaiser Wilson, Have You Forgotten Your Sympathy With the Poor Germans Because They Were Not Self-Governed? 20,000,000 American Women Are Not Self-Governed. Take the Beam Out of Your Own Eye."[7]

The Sentinels were led by Alice Paul,* who had

* Alice Paul is another New Jersey hero. Interesting note, by the way, every state is allowed two statues to display in the US Capitol. Alice Paul is not currently one of ours—but I believe she should be. CC: my dear colleagues in the New Jersey State Legislature.

broken away from the National Woman Suffrage Association—which favored a more traditional, less militant approach—to form the National Woman's Party.

As they stood outside the White House, six days a week, in the heat of summer and in the cold of winter, in the rain and in the snow, their numbers grew.[8]

Their protest was groundbreaking. It was creative, unexpected, and bold. And it provoked a firestorm of backlash.

Crowds jeered, spit on them, even pelted them with rotten food and rocks. After the United States entered World War I, they were accused of embarrassing the president and the nation during a time of crisis. Six months after the protests began, the first Sentinels were arrested. When they were taken to jail, they asked what they were being charged with. The police did not have an answer. Hours later, they were told they were being charged with "obstructing the traffic" (something those gathered to jeer and torment them were guilty of, not them). But this wasn't about justice, it was about silencing these women. As the arrests continued, they were eventually charged, convicted, and sentenced to jail.[9]

The Silent Sentinels were not deterred. Again and again, they returned to the gates of the White House, and again and again, they were arrested, charged, convicted, and given longer and longer sentences in an infamous jail, the Occoquan Workhouse, about twenty miles southwest of the White House in Virginia.

The conditions at Occoquan were filthy and brutal. Prisoners were beaten and fed bug-infested food.[10] In protest of this inhumanity, Alice Paul and others launched hunger strikes—years before Gandhi would popularize the tactic. In retaliation, guards force-fed them, ramming tubes down their throats and up their noses, pumping raw eggs into their stomachs.[11] For her refusal to relent, Paul was eventually sent to the jail's psychopathic ward, becoming part of a long tradition of powerful, unbowed woman labeled "mad."[12]

As more jailed suffragists joined the hunger strikes, news of their suffering was smuggled out and printed in papers across the country. The brutal details—beatings, force-feedings, and the women's deteriorating health—sparked national outrage.

Three weeks into Alice Paul's strike, with thirty women refusing food and eight in serious decline, the Wilson administration capitulated, releasing the women. As the suffragist Doris Stevens wrote, "The Administration . . . could not afford to feed thirty women forcibly and risk the social and political consequences; nor could it let thirty women starve themselves to death, and likewise take the consequences. For by this time, one thing was clear, and that was that the discipline and endurance of the women could not be broken."[13]

But the Silent Sentinels weren't done. They continued to press President Wilson—first to support a vote in the House on the suffrage amendment and then to push the Senate to act. They traveled the country telling their story, wearing their prison uniforms as they recounted the horrors they had endured. Their tour, known as the Prison Special, captured headlines nationwide. Cables of protest flooded the White House, demanding action. Two years after they had first stood silently outside its gates, their tremendous sacrifice finally paid off: President Wilson secured the votes needed to pass the amendment. These women didn't just move public opinion. They moved a president.[14]

* * *

SEVENTY-THREE YEARS after Alice Paul and dozens of others stood silently in front of the White House, an eight-year-old girl named Jennifer Keelan-Chaffins sat in her wheelchair down the National Mall facing the steps of the United States Capitol. She was there for the Wheels for Justice march, a protest calling for the passage of the Americans with Disabilities Act. Jennifer climbed out of her wheelchair and joined her fellow protesters ascending the Capitol steps, using her arms to lift herself up, step by step, briefly resting her chin on the marble steps as she pulled her legs up behind her.

"The people united will never be defeated" was Jennifer's favorite protest chant growing up. "To me," she said, "that meant that everyone could be included in our cause for freedom and equality, because everyone's voice matters, and so everyone has the possibility to create."

I had the privilege to speak with both Jennifer and her mom and caregiver Cynthia. They are two of the extraordinary leaders in the disability rights movement whose courage forced Congress to find its own. Today, Jennifer continues to use her voice to speak out as an advocate for Americans with disabilities.

Jennifer was six years old when the nation's first comprehensive civil rights legislation for Americans with disabilities was introduced in Congress in 1988. She had already been told she couldn't go to the same school as her sister because she was in a wheelchair. She had already been told she couldn't get on the public bus in her neighborhood because the wheelchair ramps installed on the bus, only for appearance's sake, had been manipulated to prevent anyone from actually using them. She had already been told that she couldn't join her family for dinner at a popular restaurant because her disability might make others uncomfortable. She had endured indignity after indignity, insult after insult. For her, enough was enough.

For Jennifer and millions of other Americans with disabilities, the Americans with Disabilities Act represented a promise still unfulfilled. To build support for the bill, polio survivor and disability rights activist Justin Dart hosted forums in all fifty states as well as Puerto Rico, DC, and Guam to give people with disabilities the opportunity to share their testimony. He collected thousands of stories in a "discrimination diary" that publicly documented the inequalities and indignities that people with disabilities were forced to face every day in school, at work, when voting, and in places of public accommodation.[15] This grassroots movement ushered in bipartisan support for the bill, leading to its passage in the Senate in September of 1989. But the bill stalled in the House of Representatives after an intense lobbying campaign by business organizations concerned about costs and the potential for litigation.[16] After six months of congressional inaction, disability rights activists put a new plan into motion.

On March 12, 1990, Jennifer, her mother, and her sister joined over one thousand people in the Wheels for Justice march from the White House to the Capitol. There, movement leaders and lawmakers delivered speeches from the steps of the Capitol. But then came the moment that would sear itself into the nation's consciousness. As organized by ADAPT, a disability rights organization, dozens of protesters left behind their wheelchairs, canes, and crutches and climbed the Capitol steps. They began to crawl, some with copies of the Declaration of

Independence in their pockets. Some climbed backward. Others dragged themselves forward, their faces inches from the stone where lawmakers walked. Elbows and knees scraped and bloodied, they pulled themselves up step by step—until they reached the Capitol doors.

Before the demonstration began, some of the organizers had been insistent that Jennifer should not participate, worried about the kind of message it would send for a child to be involved.[17] Jennifer later told me these concerns upset her. She had experienced the same discrimination the adults had and wanted the same chance to challenge it. She made her case to one of the leaders of ADAPT, Wade Blank, that someone from her generation needed to be represented in the demonstration. Wade listened, told her she needed to do what was in her heart, and then told her mom, who was also concerned about Jennifer's participation, to turn around, walk with him away from Jennifer, and not look back. The next thing they heard were cheers—Jennifer had abandoned her wheelchair and was now climbing up the steps of the Capitol. The press surrounded her, this eight-year-old girl with stubborn resolve and defiant determination. As cameras crowded her, she slowly ascended and declared, "I'll take all night if I have to."

What became known as the Capitol Crawl made national headlines, with photos of Jennifer crawling up the steps featured prominently, an eight-year-old girl successfully calling to the conscience of her country. Our nation and Congress were forced to see the everyday barriers people with disabilities faced. Remarkably, just a little over four months later, the Americans with Disabilities Act was signed into law.[18]

The creativity and courage of those activists didn't just shake the nation out of indifference, they created a new possibility for unity. As Jennifer later said, they did what the civil rights movement had done before: They forced America to confront the gap between its values and its reality. And in doing so, they gave our country a chance to reaffirm those values, together.

By creatively interrupting indifference, they awakened collective empathy. They called people in. They brought people together. Their actions were a force multiplier that then pushed Congress to act.

* * *

IN AN increasingly digital world, we must also fiercely prioritize physical proximity and real human connection. This isn't just vital for our individual humanity. It is vital for our politics and for our national soul. For building a more beloved community, presence matters. The call to creativity must increasingly center on meaningful, face-to-face connection. We need more morally imaginative conversations and activism *offline*. Because there is extraordinary power in showing up—in real life—and even greater power in doing so with creativity, especially in a time when the absence of human connection is fueling so many of our deepest national challenges.

Arthur Brooks, the former head of a conservative think tank, the American Enterprise Institute, has written widely about restoring connection and achieving a more united country and greater levels of well-being. He argues that face-to-face connection is not just beneficial but essential—for happiness, for meaning, for democracy itself. In a time when technology isolates us, Brooks calls us to prioritize real-world relationships—in person, in community. These connections, he says, are not luxuries. They are lifelines.[19]

These lifelines sustain our personal well-being and are also the foundation for democratic action. When we gather in real space and are truly present with one another, we create the conditions for trust, empathy, and the creative collaboration that makes change possible.

I imagine those who built the Underground Railroad, bravely meeting in secret, sharing stories and strategies, affirming shared humanity, and forging bonds strong enough to carry people to freedom. Creative activism grows from the emotional energy of proximity, from the sacred act of showing up. While online activity can be crucial to organizing, creativity in our time demands more than just being constantly online, it demands our nonviolent physicality. This physicality is powerful because it forces a reckoning, dramatizes injustice, breaks through denial, and makes the invisible visible.

That's what four Black college students in Greensboro, North Carolina, understood when they sat down at a segregated lunch counter and refused to leave. In doing so, they invented a new form of protest—nonviolent, disciplined, creative, and physical. Until segregation was challenged physically, until its ugliness was revealed through their quiet courage, too many Americans were comfortable with it. Their presence forced a confrontation. Their creative defiance broke indifference and sparked empathy.

There is something about in-person activism and engagement that strikes a deeper chord. It demands witness. It creates a shared reality no slogan, hashtag, or tweet can replicate. Our democracy needs more from us than endless posting and scrolling. It demands that we show up with creativity.

I learned this from environmental justice advocates in New Jersey and beyond who knew the civic power of public spaces and face-to-face engagement. The public square is a democratic ideal for a reason—it is the place where people can come together, connect, and be a part of the dynamism that comes from civic engagement. Advocates have long demanded that we restore and preserve public land, parks, and other community centers essential to a vibrant democracy.

When I became mayor, I was told by someone from the Trust for Public Land that Newark was one of the most underparked cities in America. So we undertook an effort to begin the largest parks expansion and rehabilitation in our city in over a century. We turned a stretch of land often used for dumping into the biggest city park. We reconnected Newark's residents, for the first time in generations, with the waterfront, reclaiming a vital artery of community. We worked with activists and nonprofits to transform acres of our city into urban gardens that grew tens of thousands of pounds of farm-fresh food.[20] In Newark's South Ward, we turned an entire city block into an urban farm. What we saw at that farm was revolutionary—a food desert vanished, an outdoor classroom opened and brought students together to learn about the earth, and a place of intergenerational engagement reconnected people with the land and with each other.

Since getting to the Senate, I have had the chance to learn from and work with environmental justice activists who have brought defiant creativity to physical spaces that were once looked down on and discarded. One person I deeply respect in these efforts is a man named Ron

Finley, the "Gangsta Gardener" from South Central Los Angeles.

Ron refused to accept the toxic reality imposed on his community. Instead of accepting a landscape of liquor stores, fast food chains, and vacant lots—a food desert barren of any healthy food—he imagined something radically different. He grabbed a shovel. He began planting fruits and vegetables in parkway medians, vacant lots, and other neglected spaces, turning them into lush gardens. His tools were seeds, soil, and sunlight. The authorities tried to stop him. They fined him. They even issued a warrant for his arrest. But Ron kept planting.[21] And in doing so, he changed more than landscapes, he changed mindsets. His resistance took root. Artists, neighbors, and even politicians began to rally behind him.

Ron said during his TED Talk in 2013,

> *See, I have a legacy in South Central. I grew up there. I raised my sons there. And I refuse to be a part of this manufactured reality that was manufactured for me by some other people and I'm manufacturing my own reality. Gardening is my graffiti. I grow my art. . . . I have witnessed my garden become a tool for the education, a tool for the transformation of my neighborhood.*
>
> *To change the community, you have to change the composition of the soil. We are the soil. . . . If you want*

> *to meet, don't call me if you want to sit around in cushy chairs and have meetings where you talk about doing some shit. . . . If you want to meet with me, come to the garden with your shovel so we can plant some shit.*[22]

Ron challenged lazy assumptions about his neighborhood. He unleashed his artistic activism and sparked a movement that brought joy, health, agency, and purpose to a place too many had written off. Albert Einstein said, "Imagination is more important than knowledge. For knowledge is limited, whereas imagination embraces the entire world, stimulating progress, giving birth to evolution."[23] Alice Paul, Jennifer Keelan-Chaffins, and Ron Finley show us that imagination, or creativity, not only embraces the world, it can transform it.

8

PERSEVERANCE

. . . the best way out is always through.

—Robert Frost, "A Servant to Servants"

THE SENATE CHAMBER IS ONE OF OUR NATION'S most sacred civic spaces. Each desk is a monument to the history that came before. After the British burned the Capitol in 1814, new desks were crafted in 1819.[1] The desks in the Senate chamber curve in a *U*, rising in tiers like an old theater. As new states joined the Union, more desks were added, each meticulously modeled after those originals. They're relics of another age: fitted with storage space for quills, tiny glass inkwells, and boxes that once contained blotting sand used to dry ink quickly.

Before leaving office, many senators write or even scratch their names into the desk drawers, tagging their temporary territory, leaving their marks to be seen by future senators who will one day leave their own. I recognize a few of the names in my own drawer, but not most. A good, humbling reminder that even if our deeds matter, our names will likely fade.

My desk, #3, happens to be one of the Senate's candy drawers—a few desks scattered through the chamber unofficially stocked with sweets.[2] Technically, food isn't allowed on the floor. Milk and water are permitted, delivered by Senate pages, impressive teenagers who remind me daily that the future is always watching. But the rules have relaxed, and discrete snacking is tolerated. I keep my drawer filled with M&Ms—a great New Jersey invention—and I take pride that my desk is a popular pit stop for colleagues.

The current chamber was completed in 1859, two years before the Civil War. Before that, senators met just down the hall, in what we now call the Old Senate Chamber. It's smaller, more intimate, and, these days, used mostly for ceremonies and a stop on Capitol tours.

Every tour guide pauses at the desk of Senator Charles Sumner, the abolitionist who was viciously beaten unconscious on that floor in 1856 for speaking out against slavery. The room is dimly lit to mimic candlelight, and all the desks are clear except Sumner's, upon which lies a book, marking the spot where conviction met cruelty.

Between that chamber and this one, the full sweep of the Senate's history has unfolded. From slavery to suffrage, war to peace, economic collapse to bold renewal. Since the ratification of the Constitution, 2,018 people have served in this body.[3] I am number 1,948.

The Senate, once drawing narrowly from a privileged few, is growing more diverse. I am only the fourth Black person ever popularly elected to this chamber. The first was Edward Brooke in 1966. The second, Carol Moseley Braun, in 1992. The third, Barack Obama, in 2004.

The first woman elected was Hattie Caraway in 1932. And though women have now served for nearly a century, they still make up only about 3 percent of all who have held a Senate seat.[4] The numbers are rising, but slowly. And yet with each new class, another "first" often breaks through. Recently, my friend and fellow Jersey Senator Andy Kim became the first Korean American elected to the Senate. These are small steps on a long road toward a chamber that more fully reflects the nation it serves.

If you look up in the Senate chamber, four Latin phrases are etched above its doors. Above the east door: *Annuit Coeptis*—"God favors our undertakings." Above the west: *Novus Ordo Seclorum*—"A new order of the ages." Over the south: our national motto—*In God We Trust*.[5] These elevated phrases serve as reminders: Service requires both reverence and resolve; leadership requires both a sense of audacity and a sense of awe. But the one that anchors me most sits high above the presiding officer's chair, facing the chamber like a quiet hope and urgent command: *E Pluribus Unum*. "Out of many, one."

The presiding officer who sits beneath those immortal words is usually a junior senator from the majority party. They take turns in shifts of an hour or so, helping the chamber move through the day's proceedings. But on rare occasions, when the vote is tied or the moment historic, the vice president of the United States steps in to preside.

On one such day, April 7, 2022, we were voting on the nomination of Judge Ketanji Brown Jackson to the Supreme Court. A brilliant jurist already confirmed multiple times by the Senate, she had served as both a district and an appellate judge. She now stood on the threshold of becoming the first Black woman in American history to serve as an associate justice of the United States Supreme Court.

That day, Vice President Kamala Harris held the gavel.

I glanced up toward the packed gallery: families, staff, citizens, children, and press gathered expectantly, eager to witness a moment that would resound through generations. Then I looked around at my colleagues milling about, waiting. Our names will most likely be forgotten, but this moment will not. This judge. This milestone. This historic stride forward.

* * *

STRETCHING HUNDREDS of feet above the Hudson River, the towering cliffs of the New Jersey Palisades have a rich history. The Lenape people who first inhabited

New Jersey—and whose descendants now make up the Nanticoke Lenni-Lenape Nation based in southern New Jersey—called the cliffs *Wee-Awk-En*, or "rocks that look like trees."[6] The cliffs were the site of at least eighteen duels between 1700 and 1884—including between Alexander Hamilton and Aaron Burr.[7] And a 1914 film serial shot with the cliffs as its backdrop is said to have popularized the term *cliffhanger*.[8]

The New Jersey Palisades are also, as Peter Brannen in *The New York Times* put it, "monuments to an apocalypse."[9] Roughly two hundred million years ago, the Palisades emerged during a series of massive volcanic eruptions that occurred as the supercontinent Pangea broke apart.[10] A group of scientists have concluded that this same volcanic activity was also likely responsible for the mass extinction event that preceded the dinosaurs and wiped out three-quarters of life on earth.[11]

In November of 1776, this spot of geological perseverance was also where, for George Washington, the American Revolution reached one of its darkest hours.[12]

Only months earlier, the members of the Second Continental Congress had adopted the Declaration of Independence. But as the patriots declared liberty, a massive British armada commanded by General William Howe advanced toward New York City. It was "the greatest military expedition any European power had ever sent overseas," Jack D. Warren Jr. told David M. Rubenstein in *The American Story*.[13]

The British struck swiftly. Washington's army suffered a devastating defeat in the Battle of Long Island.[14] Cornered in Brooklyn Heights by superior British numbers, Washington made a desperate decision. Under cover of a providential fog, he led a retreat across the East River to Manhattan.[15]

But the British kept coming, and American revolutionaries were cut down across New York. Soon, Fort Washington, located at the north end of Manhattan, was the last foothold the Continental Army held in the city. Washington believed it would be better to abandon the fort, but its commander convinced him it could hold. He relented. It was a miscalculation.[16] On November 16, British forces and Hessian mercenaries descended upon Fort Washington.[17]

From the New Jersey Palisades, Washington watched in horror as his soldiers were overwhelmed within hours. "Through his telescope he could see some of his troops fighting bravely, only to be driven back and defeated. The worst of it was to watch them surrender and see some of them put to the sword," David Hackett Fischer writes in *Washington's Crossing*. "As the full weight of the disaster fell upon him, he turned to his lieutenants and began to weep 'with the tenderness of a child.'"[18] The fort fell, and over 2,800 Americans were captured.[19]

After taking Fort Washington, British troops quickly crossed the Hudson and began scaling the cliffs of the Palisades to attack Fort Lee. Washington ordered an immediate evacuation. His troops fled so hastily, as historian David McCullough writes in *1776*, that "everything was to be left behind, guns, stores, hundreds of tents, even breakfast cooking on the fire."[20]

The battered army retreated across New Jersey into Pennsylvania, hounded by defeat. Of a force of more than twenty thousand men at the war's outset, three thousand remained.[21] Many lacked shoes, and one officer wrote of the bloody footprints they left in the snow.[22] They were cold, starving, and demoralized.

The revolution seemed all but over.

In mid-December, Washington wrote to his brother John Augustine, "Between you and me, I think our Affairs are in a very bad situation . . . If every nerve is not strained to recruit the New Army with all possible expedition, I think the game is pretty near up. . . ."[23]

Toward the end of the letter, he offered a candid confession: "You can form no Idea of the perplexity of my Situation. No Man, I believe, ever had a greater choice of difficulties, and less means to extricate himself from them."

In the depths of impossible odds, drowning amid waves of grief and loss, with ongoing trials of suffering and deprivation, Washington could have justifiably ended his letter with those despairing words. But he added another sentence: "However, under a full persuasion of the justice of our Cause I cannot entertain an Idea that it will finally sink tho' it may remain for some time under a Cloud."

* * *

Decades before she made history, eighteen-year-old Ketanji Brown Jackson sat in her dorm, a thousand miles from home, dauntingly alone.

In her memoir, *Lovely One*, she recalls arriving as a freshman at Harvard, feeling like an outsider. She hadn't come from a prestigious prep school in the Northeast like many of her classmates. She was the proud product of Florida public schools. To prepare for the bitter Massachusetts winter, she and her mother had traveled to Washington, DC, to stock up on coats, sweaters, boots, scarves, and socks.[24]

But no amount of preparation could insulate her from the chill of isolation.

One cold fall evening, walking across campus, missing her family, she felt the weight of expectation and the shadow of self-doubt pressing down on her. She later described it as "a sense of desolation unlike anything I had known before."[25] Lost in thought, she looked up—and caught the gaze of a Black woman she didn't know walking toward her. As they passed, the woman slowed just long enough to look her in the eye and utter a single word: "Persevere."[26]

I first heard this story during Jackson's confirmation hearings before the Senate Judiciary Committee.

Before nominees for the Supreme Court are voted on by the full Senate, they must go through a confirmation process, lasting at least two days, that comes to a head in a series of public hearings. It is an endurance test of mind, body, and spirit.

In those hours-long hearings, each member of the Judiciary Committee has the opportunity to ask the nominee questions about their record and judicial philosophy. At least, that is what is supposed to happen.

Before the hearings, nominees often take private meetings with senators in their offices as a matter of courtesy, an opportunity to make a human connection and discuss issues of interest and concern away from the harsh glare of national cameras.

A lot of work goes into preparing for those meetings. For my meeting with Justice Jackson, my staff on the Judiciary Committee, extraordinarily talented lawyers who have chosen public service over more lucrative endeavors, read and reviewed the judge's entire body of work, from judicial opinions to law review articles to public speeches and other writings. They solicited input from legal experts, civil rights organizations, and even some of my favorite law professors.

During my meeting with Justice Jackson, my staff and I were blown away by her towering intellect, the depth of her knowledge, and the breadth of her perspective on the law. But there was something more to her. In Ketanji Brown Jackson lies what you hope would be represented on the highest court in our land: strength, decency, and virtue.

I admit I was naïve; I allowed my expectations for a civil confirmation hearing to be raised after numerous conversations with Republican colleagues who had met with Judge Jackson and had privately expressed an impression of her that was similar to mine—she was an extraordinary human being. I allowed myself some degree of satisfaction from hearing them say things such as, *Wow, she is so impressive. She has a way about her that is truly striking and remarkable. I really liked her.*

It was clear to me that they wouldn't vote for her, but I thought it was a good sign that the hearings would be respectful.

And yet, her nomination hearings in the Judiciary Committee quickly turned ugly.

This woman of extraordinary grace was met with ruthless gracelessness.

This judge with a towering intellect was forced to endure some of the lowest, most disrespectful conduct I have ever witnessed in the United States Senate.

It wasn't all of my Republican colleagues, but some of them used her hearing as a platform to hurl misleading, demeaning, and degrading attacks.

Senator Ted Cruz of Texas asked Judge Jackson if she believed "that babies are racist." With a question that provoked America's grievance-laden culture wars instead of probing Judge Jackson's actual judicial record—later garnering the senator widespread praise in conservative media—Senator Marsha Blackburn of Tennessee asked the judge to define the word *woman*. Senator Josh Hawley of Missouri accused Judge Jackson of "a pattern of letting child porn offenders off the hook for their appalling crime." The conservative *National Review* called Senator Hawley's allegation "meritless to the point of demagoguery" and referred to his implication that Judge Jackson was somehow soft on sex offenders as a "smear."[27]

The energy in the hearing room grew dark and heavy. It felt suffocating. Instead of being celebrated as a historic nominee, Judge Jackson found her dignity being tested in public.

Each time she was pushed, disrespected, or spoken down to, she maintained her poise and demonstrated an incredible level of restraint. I, however, was finding it almost impossible to witness. While she sat stoically, I could barely contain myself. For me, it was impossible not to see my mother, my cousins, and my ancestors in this woman. Like her, they had endured insult after insult, often from men grossly less qualified than them. Yet somehow they had managed to succeed in a world that had repeatedly failed to recognize their worth.

Meanwhile, my phone was blowing up as friends and family (somehow unable to see that I was working and was not supposed to be on my phone) felt compelled to express their horror. They were watching as countless stations, news outlets, and social media platforms showed America the split screen: one side, angry senators, on the attack; the other, Justice Jackson's unwavering, quiet dignity and resolve.

Finally, it was my turn to speak. Justice Jackson had endured hours of indignities. I wanted her to have a moment of rest. So I told her I had no questions, just some things I wanted to say.

I told her that I was disappointed, though not surprised, by the treatment she had received and that she had shown grit and grace in response. I told her that she had earned that seat. I said the obvious: "You have earned this spot, you are worthy, you are a great American," I told her.

And I spoke of Harriet Tubman, who, despite all she endured, never once stopped going back to help others escape, never stopped believing in freedom, never stopped looking up. I told Judge Jackson, amidst her master class in perseverance, that I looked up to her, that she was in fact my North Star. That on that day, amidst the darkness, she was a guiding light for so many Americans who are enduring their own unjust challenges.

I told her that, despite all the attacks and verbal assaults, no one would steal my joy. Not for this moment. They couldn't tarnish this triumph. I told her she wasn't alone sitting there. I told her about the middle-aged Black woman who had stopped me on my run that morning—nearly tackled me in the street—just to say what it meant to her to see Jackson in that seat. "You tell Judge Jackson that we're standing with her," she had said to me.

For fifteen minutes, I unapologetically broke usual senatorial decorum and deference, as my angry Republican colleagues had done. I got personal. I got emotional. My voice broke as I spoke to her. As I wrapped up, I told her, "Don't worry, my sister, don't worry. God has got you. And how do I know that? You're here, and I know what it's taken for you to sit in that seat." When I finished, I sat back, exhausted. And I felt relieved. The suffocatingly dense air was gone. I could breathe. And I noticed that this poised federal judge—who had endured so much, for so long—allowed herself a single tear.[28]

Mercifully, Senator Dick Durbin of Illinois, the chairman of the committee, banged the gavel and said, in essence, that we all needed a brief recess. What happened next surprised me. The notoriously colorful and sometimes cantankerous Senator John Kennedy, a Republican from Louisiana and an actual across-the-aisle friend, hustled over to me, and before my staff could lean in with any comments or, as is often the case, critiques, he grabbed me by the hand and told me, with a sense of gratitude, that he found my words moving.

The moment I found most moving was later, during questioning from my friend, Senator Alex Padilla of California. It was then that Judge Jackson shared the story of that woman who once looked her in the eye and said just one word: "Persevere." And in a high-stakes Senate confirmation hearing, Ketanji Brown Jackson did.

That single whispered word—*persevere*—that comforted her as a lonely freshman carried with it the weight of generations who had walked through hardship, pain, trial, and exclusion.

We all face difficult moments, times when we feel overwhelmed, isolated, and alone—stressed, anxious, and in over our heads, as if we are not capable or worthy. We face relentless demands, suffocating costs, and traps of life that drag us into doubt and despair. And yet, in describing the depths of her struggle, she named our common truth: We all falter, we all doubt, we all encounter winters where we wonder if we can make it through. Ketanji Brown Jackson—on the highest platform, aiming for the highest court—met us where we are, in our common humanity. Her one-word message was a testimony and a charge to all. *Persevere.*

* * *

THE DAY finally came for Ketanji Brown Jackson's full Senate vote. As the last votes were being cast, I couldn't sit still at my desk. I began pacing in the back of the chamber. I was feeling the power of the moment, and I confess, I was emotional, again. My staff jokes that I can have only one public cry a month, and I was told before I went to the Senate floor that day that I had already exceeded my monthly allotment.

As I walked back and forth like an expectant father from a 1950s movie, the good Reverend Doctor Senator Raphael Warnock of Georgia, a man who has more titles than the Newark Public Library, approached me.

"Brother Booker, you OK? Seems like you are struggling," he said.

I laughed. "Brother Warnock, I need some prayer," I told him. As he and I beamed at the meaning of the moment, a determined staffer came over to us and, with a sense of hurry, deference, and a hint of command, informed us, "Senators, the presiding officer would like to see you."

Both Warnock and I knew that when the vice president of the United States calls you, you immediately go. And we had both been conditioned since we were little boys to know that when a Black woman calls you over, you rush to them and say, "Yes, ma'am." So, with a double dose of urgency, we hustled over to the presiding officer.

Now, a delightful truth I was once told about the presiding officer of the Senate is that when you go to speak to them, you should not stand next to them. The presiding officer is the highest person in that body, literally, so you are supposed to lean over or crouch. So as the two of us got to the vice president, we both kneeled on the steps as if we were about to receive communion.

Vice President Kamala Harris greeted us. The joy we were all feeling was evident. All of us were high on history. The vice president said it plainly: "This is a historic moment, gentlemen."

In addition to the already historic nature of the day, the three of us, gathered there together, were in our own way making a bit of history. This was the first time three Black people had gathered together on the Senate floor, all of whom had served as senators, and one of them was now vice president of the United States.

But the high of history we were all feeling wasn't about that. Ketanji Brown Jackson was breaking a barrier. And now the first woman vice president was determined that we two senators should do something special to mark this moment.

She suggested that we each write a letter to a little girl we know, to tell her what this moment means to us and to them, and that we should do it right then, while we were waiting.

Before either of us could get a word out, as if to impress upon us the import of this assignment, she flipped open her leather-bound folder containing her schedule and other important papers for her day. From the back pocket, she pulled the last two remaining pieces of blank paper, handing one to each of us. I grabbed mine from her and there it was, her own stationery, bearing a golden embossed seal and "The Vice President." The rest of the page was blank.

Write your letter to that little girl using my stationery, she had said.

One public cry, only one public cry! I silently reminded myself. I braced myself against Warnock for strength as I imagined him saying firmly, *Don't cry, Booker! Dammit! Don't you cry! Jesus, help this poor man!*

Warnock is a disciplined, dedicated man. He went back to his desk and wrote out a letter to his six-year-old daughter. It is a beautiful letter that he fortunately later shared publicly. "Dear Chloé," he writes,

> Today, we confirmed Ketanji Brown Jackson to the United States Supreme Court. In our nation's history, she is the first Supreme Court Justice who looks like you—with hair like yours. While we were voting on the floor of the Senate, a friend of mine, the Vice President of the United States, handed me this piece of paper and suggested I write a note to someone who comes to mind. By the way, she is the first Vice President who also looks like you! So, I write this to say you can be anything, achieve anything you set your head and heart to do. Love you! Dad[29]

As for me, I was back at my desk. Sitting. Spinning. Procrastinating. I have no daughter. I couldn't decide whom to write the letter to. One of my nieces, my cousins, the daughter of a dear friend, my future child? I was stuck. And what should I write? What should I say? And then, it was too late. The last of the hundred senators to vote leaned in from the Republican Cloakroom off the Senate floor and voted no. The final vote count was in. Ketanji Brown Jackson was confirmed. Kamala Harris announced the tally, 53–47. The chamber erupted. Rules were ignored and people applauded from the gallery and on the floor.

I celebrated with others and left the Senate floor with my blank stationery.

I'd missed the moment. As if I were back in college, a paralyzing mix of procrastination, writer's block, and overwhelm had prevailed. But I protected that paper. I secured it in a binder and carried it back to my office. The assignment still compelled. I couldn't stop thinking about the vice president's words. Write a letter. As days passed, then weeks, the assignment still called to me.

"What would you write?" I asked others. And the more I thought and listened, I began to realize that we are all here because of letters written by our ancestors. Not letters with ink and pen but with tears and sweat and blood.

What we do every day is our letter. How we live, how we show up is our lasting testimony to those who will come after us. Kamala Harris had given me an assignment: "Write your letter." But this is only a symbol or metaphor for the living assignment we all have. What letter are we writing with our lives?

This book is some of the work I've done on the assignment. And here is what I would have liked to have written in the moment, and perhaps one day what I will actually give, God willing, to a daughter of my own, on stationery given to me by a historic vice president on a day in which a historic Supreme Court justice was confirmed to the court.

Beloved,

I write this letter to you on the occasion of Justice Ketanji Brown Jackson's confirmation to the Supreme Court of the United States. I write it under the instruction of, and with paper handed to me by the Vice President of the United States, Kamala Harris.

This is a moment overflowing with joy. Another affirmation of our country's promise being made real. I wish I could tell you the work is now done, that we secured justice, achieved peace, and made this union truly perfect. But we have not. This is a milestone, not the mountaintop. There is still so much to do.

And you, my dear one, like our nation, will face trials. You will witness injustice and most likely experience it too. You will carry pain not of your making. You will undoubtedly endure winters of despair. And you will confront challenges—some passed down by my generation, others born of your own.

Yet, as Justice Jackson showed in her journey to the bench, your character, and the character of our country, will not be defined by what happens to you but by how you choose to respond.

So I urge you—respond with grit. Respond with grace. Most of all, respond with love.

And remember that even when you think you are standing alone, you are not. An unbroken chain stretching back to before the founding of this country belongs to you now, an unconquerable, indomitable, invincible perseverance. This is your inheritance.

Persevere, my beloved, persevere.

* * *

THE APPROPRIATELY named Military Park sits in Newark's downtown, just a couple of miles from where I live. During the Civil War, Union soldiers were recruited in the park. It was used as a campground for soldiers during the War of 1812. During World War I, the park served as both a recruiting station and a location where Americans could donate to the Red Cross and purchase Liberty Bonds to help fund the American war effort.[30] Eight years after World War I, a sprawling monument was erected there. The sculpture was intended to honor all the American war dead. It was also built as a tribute to all the Americans who answered the call to arms, including so many who answered in that very park.

This park was first used for American military purposes during the darkest days of the Revolution. General Washington and the beleaguered American troops retreating from the British across New Jersey camped there just days after the capture of Fort Washington. Among them was Thomas Paine, an English immigrant who, earlier that year, had published his pamphlet *Common Sense*, arguing for the creation of a new nation, independent from the British. As *Common Sense* found widespread popularity, so did support for revolution. Historians credit Paine's work as vital to rallying early Americans to the cause of revolution and strengthening American perseverance in the face of the imposing British forces.[31]

Now serving as a volunteer aide to Major General Nathanael Greene, Paine was camped out in Newark, New Jersey, in Military Park, when he put his pen to paper and began work on what would later become a new pamphlet, *The American Crisis*.[32]

The most famous words from that pamphlet, written during a desperate retreat and surrounded by the wavering spirit of beaten men, are the first:

> THESE are the times that try men's souls. The summer soldier and the sunshine patriot will, in this crisis, shrink from the service of their country; but he that stands it now, deserves the love and thanks of man and woman. Tyranny, like hell, is not easily conquered; yet we have this consolation with us, that the harder the conflict,

> the more glorious the triumph. What we obtain too cheap, we esteem too lightly: it is dearness only that gives every thing its value.[33]

The American Crisis was published less than a month later, on December 19, 1776, in *The Pennsylvania Journal.* According to historian David Hackett Fischer, "It traveled through the country as fast as galloping horses could carry it. Within a day of its first publication it was circulating in the camps of the Continental army along the Delaware River."[34] Less than a week later, on Christmas night, General Washington crossed the Delaware back into New Jersey, in what still is perhaps the most famous river crossing in American history. He led his troops in a surprise attack on the Hessian and British camps. Their victory in Trenton would be the first for the Continental Army and would mark a turning point for the Revolution.

Paine's letter to America renewed the morale of an army and a nation.

Today, almost two and a half centuries later, the first sentences of that pamphlet are still something of an American anthem. But my favorite part comes toward the end.

Written at the very dawn of America, it remains an enduring message of perseverance: "Let it be told to the future world, that in the depth of winter, when nothing but hope and virtue could survive, that the city and the country, alarmed at one common danger, came forth to meet and to repulse it. . . . By perseverance and fortitude we have the prospect of a glorious issue."[35]

9

GRACE

No one is as capable of gratitude as one who has emerged from the kingdom of night. We know that every moment is a moment of grace, every hour an offering; not to share them would mean to betray them. Our lives no longer belong to us alone; they belong to all those who need us desperately.

—Elie Wiesel, Nobel Prize acceptance speech, December 10, 1986

IMAGINE A NIGHTMARE PLANE RIDE: YOU'RE stuck in the window seat, and the person beside you simply will not stop talking. That is where the great statesman John Lewis found himself in January of 2019, except he was on a two-and-a-half-hour drive through Georgia and his companion was a very curious and very persistent United States senator from New Jersey.

This was the road trip of my life. But in retrospect, for

John, it must have felt even worse than getting stuck next to a chatty stranger on an airplane because I already knew so much about his life *and* I had a lot of questions.

John Lewis was my hero—the man had led Freedom Rides, countless demonstrations, and marches, had been the youngest speaker at the March on Washington, and had been beaten, arrested dozens of times, jailed, and still kept showing up, speaking up, standing up, and causing, in his words, "good trouble."

I listened intently as he told stories and shared wisdom—never faltering in his insistence on the redemptive power of leading with love and with grace. At one point, I may or may not have launched into an extremely leading question. I painted a disturbing picture of where we found ourselves at that moment: The Supreme Court had gutted the Voting Rights Act—the very law he had bled for. The president then—as he does again today—openly praised dictators, modeled authoritarian behavior, and mastered a meanness in speech, in tweets, and in actions. Threats against public officials on both sides of the aisle were rising. Political violence and threats of violence were becoming more common. Tribalism was deepening and hardening. And cruelty had become fashionable and was celebrated and elevated as an acceptable political strategy. I spoke of the erosion of vital democratic norms, the confusion of justice with vengeance, the rise in inequality, and the flood of dark money unleashed by the Supreme Court's *Citizens United* decision further drowning out the voices of everyday Americans. As I laid it all out, John listened quietly. I finally asked my question: How did he cope with the weight of it all? How did he hold to his values in the face of so much backsliding in our nation?

John didn't try to soften my critique or placate me. He didn't deny the present darkness. He was blunt—and clearly angry—about the state of our nation, so he didn't hide his pain at what we were witnessing. He wasn't afraid to name the immorality and deep dysfunction of our time, just as he had done decades earlier. For John, truth telling was always essential, especially when so many were trying to deny, distort, or cover up the suffering of others.

John also did not take me up on the opportunity to fan the flames of my outrage. He spoke instead about something more difficult, more powerful, more strategic: grace.

The movement John helped lead faced relentless cruelty—but it refused to mirror it. In the face of violence, hatred, and dehumanization, they did not adopt the tactics of their adversaries. They modeled a better way. A braver way. A more effective way to fight and win.

Violence is seductive. When someone strikes you and

assaults your dignity, your instinct is to strike back. But John Lewis's life was a case study in the active rejection of that instinct and the triumph of grace. "Someone beats you, spits on you, throws you in jail—you still love them. Just love the hell out of everybody," he told me. "Love is not weak. Love is strong. Whatever you do, do it in a peaceful, orderly, nonviolent way, in the spirit of love. Get in good trouble. Make a little noise. We have the right to protest for what is right."

This wasn't theoretical for John. He told me the story of how, in May of 1961, he and twelve others had boarded buses in Washington, DC, bound for New Orleans. They were Freedom Riders—seven Black, six white—testing a Supreme Court ruling that outlawed segregation in interstate travel. When they reached Rock Hill, South Carolina, John and two others tried to enter a whites-only waiting room. They were brutally attacked by a waiting mob.

"He hit me in the face," John said of the man who beat him. "Knocked me down. I thought I was going to die."

To the surprise of many, John and the others never pressed charges, despite being given the chance to do so. They just got back on the bus.

Then, John said, nearly fifty years later, the man who beat him—Elwin Wilson, a former Klansman—walked into his congressional office in Washington, DC. It turned out that Wilson's beating of Lewis wasn't an isolated act. He had been a violent white supremacist for years: a member of the Klan who hung a Black doll from a noose outside his home, participated in cross burnings, and attacked his Black neighbors.[1]

Shortly after President Obama's election, and just four years before Wilson's death, he called a local paper. He said he wanted to apologize. He said that for years, he knew that what he had done was wrong. And he specifically wanted to find the man he had beaten so badly at the Rock Hill bus station.

He learned that man was now a US congressman—John Lewis. So, he traveled to Washington, DC, with his son and stepped into Congressman Lewis's office.

He said he was sorry. And he asked John for his forgiveness.

John paused as he told this part of the story.

So I asked him, "When the man who had beaten you, who cracked your bones and spilled your blood, came back decades later and asked for forgiveness—what did you do?"

He looked me straight in the eyes. "I forgave him," he said. "Every one of us needs mercy. Every one of us needs redemption."

Then, he told me he hugged the man, looked at the man's son, and said, "This nation needs you too."

There was a disciplined toughness in his voice. John was a fighter. He believed in confrontation. He believed injustice had to be named, challenged, and defeated. But grace, as John modeled it, was a choice about *how* to fight. In refusing to meet darkness with more darkness, grace is a deliberate choice not to become what you are against—perhaps a harder choice but, ultimately, a more transformative one. And make no mistake—there is power in grace. Grace doesn't excuse injustice or erase history, it confronts both. Grace, John demonstrated, is how we fight injustice without becoming unjust ourselves.

* * *

IT WAS a Sunday morning, and Daniel Anderl was up in his room, talking to his mom, while his dad was making coffee downstairs. "Mom," he told her, "I have had just the best weekend ever."

Covid-19 meant that Daniel and his friends had finished their sophomore year at Catholic University studying remotely from home, and they hadn't seen each other in months. He begged his parents to let his friends come visit for his birthday, promising they would take all the necessary precautions. They finally agreed, and Daniel was overjoyed. He spent his twentieth birthday weekend at his parents' home in New Jersey surrounded by the people who loved him the most.

Daniel was his parents' only child, and after four miscarriages, they'd felt so lucky to have him. From as early as he could swing a bat, Daniel played baseball for local and travel teams and loved the game. However, Daniel decided to focus on his studies once he got to Catholic University because he wanted to become a lawyer, just like his parents.[2] He took every opportunity to tell his friends how deeply proud he was of his family—his father, Mark Anderl, a successful defense attorney, and his mother, Judge Esther Salas, the first Latina to serve as a US district court judge in the state of New Jersey.

Later that Sunday evening, Daniel was helping his mom clean up the basement when the doorbell rang. "Who is that?" he asked. He sprinted up the stairs and raced to open the door.[3]

No one knows what the man at the door—who appeared to be a deliveryman—said to Daniel or what Daniel said in response. But within moments, Daniel had extended his arms, trying to block the shooter from entering their home. He took a bullet to the chest.

The gunman then turned the gun on Mark, shooting him three times. By the time Judge Salas got to the door, the shooter was gone.

That night, as doctors worked to try to save Daniel and Mark, Judge Salas sat in a cold, sterile hospital waiting room. When Daniel's doctors finally entered, she took one look at their faces and knew what they had come to tell her. She grabbed one of the doctors and shook him. She had lost her only child just a few days after his twentieth birthday.

Her husband, though badly wounded, survived.

The FBI later told Esther and Mark that the man who had attacked their family had been stalking them all weekend. He had been watching, and waiting, as Daniel's friends had come and gone. The gunman, who had once argued a case before Judge Salas, described himself as an "anti-feminist lawyer" and had targeted the judge by name in a racist, misogynist, hate-filled manifesto. He had then found her home address online.

In the five years since their son's murder, Esther and Mark have dedicated themselves to honoring his life through their advocacy to protect judges and their families. They were instrumental in the introduction and passage of Daniel's Law in New Jersey, which prohibits the disclosure of the home addresses of judges and other public officials in the state. And at the national level, they championed the Daniel Anderl Judicial Security and Privacy Act, a bill I helped write and lead through the Senate. Signed into law by President Biden in December of 2022, it prohibits agencies and private businesses from publicly posting the personal information of federal judges and their immediate family members.

As they have worked to advocate for the safety of judges and their families, they have also helped open food pantries in Daniel's honor in New Jersey, Ohio, and Hawaii. The goal of the pantries is to "transform sorrow into positivity." In the pantry in New Jersey, a photo of Daniel is accompanied by the words "love is light."[4]

In the same five years since Daniel was killed, threats and heinous acts of violence against federal judges and people who serve the public across the country—from police officers to prosecutors, from teachers to election workers, and from elected officials at every level of government to members of the media and people in the public eye—have skyrocketed.

In the spring of 2025, nearly five years after Daniel's murder, Judge Salas was preparing for the opening of another food pantry in his honor when she got a phone call from a federal judge. Judges across the country were being targeted with a new type of intimidation tactic known as "pizza doxxing"—people were anonymously sending pizzas to the homes of judges and their families as both a message and a threat: *We know who you are and we know where you live.* It had already happened to this judge once, but he called Judge Salas because this time, he said, the order form had Daniel's name on it.

In the five years since Daniel's murder, his name has been used dozens of times in similar threats against federal judges. If you listen to Judge Salas talk about the memory of her son being used for such a dark purpose, you can see that she is hurt and angry. How could she not be? She not only endured the worst possible thing any parent could experience, but her deepest pain is now being used as a weapon against fellow federal judges. Yet Judge Salas finds a way to do something more difficult, something stronger than simply expressing her righteous anger—she has found a way to speak, live, and fight with grace.

The grace Judge Salas demonstrates does not excuse horrific injustice. And it is not weak—show me someone stronger than a mother whose son was stolen from her but who still insists on honoring his light and his love instead of descending into the darkness. Judge Salas speaks forcefully about the rise in political violence, threats to the independence of the judiciary, and threats to the rule of law, but she never speaks carelessly. She seeks to honor her son's life through her example, through her insistence on, as she says it, "shedding light and not heat" on the crisis of political violence. She believes that words matter—that how we speak to one another matters—and she lives that belief through her example. Again and again, when it would be completely understandable for her to choose otherwise, she chooses grace.

How?

After Daniel was murdered, Esther and Mark moved

into a rental house—it was unsafe and too painful for them to return home. On Sundays, their pastor would come over to do a private mass. One Sunday, nearly a month after Daniel's murder, their pastor was talking about faith and forgiveness as a pathway for healing. Sitting in Mark's bedroom that doubled as a makeshift hospital room, with her hand tightly gripped around her husband's, her head bowed, Esther uttered the words that would change everything for her: "God, I forgive him. God, I forgive him. God, I forgive him."

For Esther, this was the moment that her pain began to be transformed into purpose.

I know there are people who would say that it would be impossible for them to forgive the man who killed their son. But for Esther, forgiveness was not about giving something to the man who took everything from her; it was about refusing to allow him to take anything more. It was about reclaiming her power through grace. It was about defiantly holding on to the light and love her son represents.

Judge Salas shared:

> Forgiveness is not about trying to change what has happened . . . nothing can change what has happened. Forgiveness is about allowing what has happened to change you. How does it change

> you? How does forgiveness change who *you* are? I miss my son terribly . . . but I'm quickly brought back to the present moment, which is just learning to have grace. . . . I heard someone once say that [faced with] great suffering, you can either transmit it or transform it, and Mark and I have chosen to transform it.

Judge Salas believes that grace is a choice available to all of us. There is "nothing like having your only child murdered in front of you to give you perspective," she said in a podcast interview, "but I dare say that we don't need to get to that level of tragedy."[5] She believes, and she demonstrates, that we all have the capacity, every day, to choose grace, to bring forth more kindness, love, and compassion in ourselves and the world.

Grace does not preclude righteous anger. Instead, it insists that our anger be righteous. It does not ask us to stop fighting. It asks us to fight without hate. It doesn't mean we don't get weary. It means we rest, rise, and return to the work with love still intact. Grace takes guts. It demands both mental and physical toughness. Grace is both a moral choice and a strategic decision to refuse to be corrupted by hatred or injustice. Because grace, wielded with courage, threatens the very foundations of those who perpetrate injustice. When you refuse to hate your enemy, you deny them the validation and even power they crave—they no longer control you and fail in their attempts to diminish or defeat you.

* * *

ON JULY 17, 2020, John Lewis's chief of staff and rock-solid right hand for years, Michael Collins, called me.

He told me that it wouldn't be long. He told me that he knew how much we meant to each other and wanted to give me an opportunity to say goodbye. He told me that John wasn't able to speak or respond but that he would be able to hear me when I spoke.

I was caught off guard by the call. I hadn't prepared. And now the phone was put to his ear. How do you say goodbye to your hero? How do you say goodbye to the man who changed the course of your life and changed the course of our country in the moments before God calls him home?

When I was first sworn in as a senator in October of 2013 after a special election, my mom and I were in mourning. I had just lost my dad six days before the election and my mom had just lost her husband of nearly fifty years. So when we got to DC, my mom and my team arranged for us to have breakfast with John Lewis in his office; in a spiritual sense, they hoped that John could help salve the pain of the missing presence of my father.

John told my mom and me how proud he was of this moment and that he felt like this was one of the things he had fought for during his career. He told us how excited he was to be able to soon stand there on the Senate floor to watch me get sworn in. My mom wept in his office and all of us hugged.

An hour or so later, John Lewis did indeed stand right there on the Senate floor, beaming as a proud father figure while the vice president, Joe Biden, read me my oath. John Lewis and my dad, who I am sure was there in spirit, watched me raise my hand and another milestone was marked: The United States Senate was changing. My parents' and John Lewis's generation opened doors, paved roads, and made countless sacrifices; they gave their offerings and made a way for my generation to rise higher, go farther, and continue the unfinished work.

When the phone was pressed to John's ear, I tried at first to express my gratitude for all that he had done for our nation and for all that he had done for me. Then, I don't know if I found the words or the words found me. "John," I said, trying to compose my own emotion. "John, I love you. . . . John, I know where you are going, you are going home, you are going to be in Heaven looking down on us. . . . John, I promise you—I promise you that I will do everything possible, that *we* will do everything possible, to make you proud, to make you proud of us."

* * *

JUST TWO days after John Lewis's death, I received the phone call that a federal judge in New Jersey had been attacked. Her husband had been shot multiple times. Her son had been murdered.

The contrast between their deaths underscored the tragedy of Daniel's loss: John Lewis had died peacefully in his home in Atlanta, at the age of eighty, after a long life; Daniel Anderl was murdered in his home in New Jersey at the age of twenty.

But it turns out the same virtue had defined their lives. Grace. Heroic grace.

After one of Daniel's memorial services ended, one of his close friends, Joe, approached Esther. He wanted to tell her about something Daniel had said the last time they were together, when Joe had come to visit for his birthday. Daniel was driving Joe back to the airport when he said something unusual. Daniel told his friend that he knew there were people who had done his family wrong, who had done him wrong. Then, Daniel simply said, "But I forgive them."

Just a few days later, Daniel would give his life to save his parents.

Grace is not weakness. Grace is not a sign of cowardice.

It is a sign of unimaginable courage.

Grace is what fortifies us.

Yet we live in a moment when violent rhetoric and political violence are not only rising but increasingly excused, normalized, and even celebrated. Johns Hopkins professor and author Lilliana Mason, who calls political violence "at its core . . . a rejection of democracy," points out that "if the people who lead us are using violent or dehumanizing rhetoric, then it's a signal to their supporters that violent rhetoric is acceptable, and that violent action might be acceptable."[6]

This dangerous reality demands more of all of us. It demands more of every elected leader, and I say this knowing full well that I've fallen short of the mark myself. I remind myself constantly, every time I post online or speak in public, even in private conversations, of the words of Judge Salas—calling us to be "impeccable with our word."

Now is not the time to meet cruelty with careless outrage. It is time to act like what we say to each other, or post on social media, or say in front of our children matters, because it does.

Embracing and extending grace to each other and to ourselves is not easy. But it is the only path to transformation and redemption, for ourselves, our politics, and our country.

Grace is powerful. It is courageous. It is defiant.

Most of all, grace is a choice, one that is always available to us, in every moment, every day.

10

VISION

When day comes, we step out of the shade, aflame and unafraid. The new dawn blooms as we free it. For there is always light, if only we're brave enough to see it. If only we're brave enough to be it.

—Amanda Gorman, "The Hill We Climb"

The way you look at things is the most powerful force shaping your life.

—John O'Donohue

MY MOTHER NOW LIVES IN LAS VEGAS. SOME JERsey parents retire to Florida; mine moved to Sin City. Living in a retirement community in Vegas means my mom gets to exercise her special gift: an almost mystical talent for knowing which slot machine is about to hit. My grandmother had it too. Some families inherit jewelry; the women in my family apparently inherit casino instincts.

A few years ago, I took a trip to visit her—not to follow her around the casino or take her to the finest buffets in the world but for a very specific purpose. My mother had been cast in a play at her retirement community. From the moment she told me, I knew I had a sacred duty to attend. After all, she'd been present for every one of my childhood productions—whether I was a chorus member in a Christmas assembly or trying to belt out the Jets theme with braces on in my eighth grade production of *West Side Story* (yes, when you are a Jet you are indeed a Jet all the way). The karmic wheel had spun, and it was my turn to sit in the front row.

So I flew across the country to see her performance. And I didn't just sit there, I went into full embarrassing parent mode. I planted myself in the front row with my phone out, recording every moment like I was Spielberg filming a masterpiece. At one point, an octogenarian gentleman behind me leaned forward and whispered, "Thank you, young man. I'm farsighted, so I can't see the stage clearly. But I can watch the whole show on your phone. Best seat in the house."

Then came the moment that floored me. My mom, playing the role of the Red Queen in a unique rendition of *Alice Through the Looking-Glass*, sat regally with the White Queen who delivered one of the more famous lines in all of literature. Alice says, "There's no use in trying, one can't believe impossible things."[1]

And the White Queen replies: "I daresay you haven't had much practice. When I was your age, I always did it for half-an-hour a day. Why, sometimes I've believed as many as six impossible things before breakfast."

Watching my mother as that line was uttered—straight faced, in ridiculous regalia, in a Vegas retirement community, sitting next to a seventy-something woman playing Alice—was hilarious. But it was also deeply moving. Because the truth is, that was my family's story. And it is our American story.

We are a nation built by people who dared to believe the unbelievable, even when the odds were far worse and the stakes much higher than at any blackjack table. Women fighting for suffrage? That was dangerous. That was "impossible." Until it wasn't. Workers organizing for fair wages and retirement security? Many died in that fight. Impossible, until one day it was the law. Civil rights activists facing fire hoses and bombs? Impossible that they could prevail, until they did.

Our shared history, our family stories, our collective legacy is one of impossible dreams made real—as I've said before, we are our ancestors' wildest dreams. But let's not diminish their accomplishments in retrospect. They dared to dream, they had audacious hopes and courageous ambitions, *and* they backed them up with grit, sacrifice, and struggle.

Growing up, when I sat at the feet of my elders—my

grandparents, aunts, and uncles—their stories weren't tales of easy glory or effortless abundance. They spoke of struggle and setback, agony and betrayal. The heartbreak of nights when the very government that should have been protecting them was instead working against them. My mom told me stories of her childhood, waking up in the middle of the night in Detroit as someone from Louisiana had showed up on their doorstep, fleeing terror because they had violated some absurd racial code with deeply dangerous consequences. My grandparents gave them shelter for a night or two and then helped them across the border into Canada, where they would be safe.

And yet—even in the face of violence and discrimination—my family and so many others dared to believe in America. They believed in "impossible things": a better life for their children, schools that would educate instead of exclude, jobs that offered dignity to all, communities where hospitals and healthcare were open to all, neighborhoods that were safe and in which everyone's children could thrive. Our ancestors were audacious in their belief. Defiant in their dreams. This is the America we inherited.

James Baldwin captured this truth perfectly. After laying out many of America's harshest realities in his time in his 1963 book *The Fire Next Time*, he still ended with words that some thought were almost too hopeful, and critics said he was being excessive or even Pollyannaish: "I know what I'm asking is impossible. But in our time, as in every time, the impossible is the least that one can demand—and one is, after all, emboldened by the spectacle of human history in general, and the American Negro history in particular, for it testifies to nothing less than the perpetual achievement of the impossible."[2]

The perpetual achievement of the impossible. That's more than a beautiful turn of phrase. It's an urgent reminder that so much of what we now consider ordinary or even take for granted—civil rights, suffrage, public school for all children without discrimination, the forty-hour work week, marrying who you love—was once dismissed as laughably unrealistic. This is the real-life, deeply meaningful, political equivalent of believing in six impossible things before breakfast.

Our ancestors practiced believing in impossible things.

Our ancestors held strong to a bold vision of America—not as fantasy but as fuel.

Now it is our turn.

* * *

Too many are losing faith in the American idea, the American promise, and the hope that the American Dream can work for them and their families.

Americans are working harder than ever, yet wages remain mostly stagnant while the cost of everything—housing, healthcare, childcare, education—continues to rise. We are confronting a growing retirement crisis as more seniors, after working all their lives, face insecurity as their Social Security checks don't cover their basic needs. Too many parents no longer believe their children will live better lives than they did, and they see a future shaped not by promise but by uncertainty and scarcity.

The data backs up this pessimism: Someone growing up in my parents' generation had a greater than 90 percent chance of earning more than their parents did; for people born in the 1980s, that drops to just 50 percent.[3] Productivity continues to increase, but wages are not keeping pace with the work that Americans are doing. According to the Pew Research Center, over a nearly fifty-year period between 1970 and 2018, the middle class's share of income has fallen by 19 percent, while the wealthiest have increased their share of total income by 20 percent. The last time disparities in wealth had grown this bad was the eve of the Great Depression.[4]

We have distinguished ourselves on indices that no country would ever want to lead in—we are one of the world's deadliest wealthy countries for expectant and new mothers, and we have one of the highest child poverty rates among our peers. We tolerate the fact that the number one cause of death for American children and teens is gun violence. We have decided that teaching our children how to hide when a gunman enters their school is easier than asking ourselves why we can't protect them in the first place. In America, people are rushed to emergency rooms at alarming rates because they are forced to ration basic medications like insulin. Our country is also home to a deeply broken criminal justice system that widens racial disparities, punishes poverty, and criminalizes those struggling with mental health at staggering costs to taxpayers, as well as a deeply broken immigration system that both endangers our national security and betrays our values.[5]

On top of all this, fear has increasingly crept into our national story: fear of immigrants, fear of each other, fear of the future. A demagogue has risen who manipulates and manufactures this fear as currency to enrich himself and his powerful allies. Our politics are consumed by attack ads, opposition research, enemies lists, and long declarations of who is wrong, bad, or even evil.

And too often, our politicians and parties define themselves by who and what they oppose rather than who and what they stand for and what they dare to dream.

The American Dream was never just about personal ambition—it was always about shared promise. It was a bold vision rooted in humble hopes: that hard work could lead to security and prosperity, that children could rise higher than their parents, that elders would grow old with dignity, that those facing hardship would not be abandoned but embraced by a nation of grace and justice, that ultimately your worth is not defined by your wealth, your zip code, or your skin color but by your humanity, your effort, your dreams, and what you do to help others.

We must rekindle that vision. We must redeem the dream.

The vision we need now is not one of quaint nostalgia about our past or blind denial about our present but one of bold courage and daily conviction to build a better future.

And that vision starts not with the big policy debates we have in the halls of Congress but with simple truths about who we are to one another and what kind of country we choose to be.

And that brings me back to my mother.

* * *

THE ONCE Red Queen of Las Vegas and always one of the wisest and often most ruthlessly honest women I know has a knack—a gift, really—for telling stories about my faults, foibles, or embarrassing moments. This is the woman who likes to introduce me by saying, "Behind every successful child . . . is an astonished parent."

One of her favorite stories takes place back when I was about ten years old. I had chicken pox. (In my memory, it was not the mild kind, no, I had the "why is the universe punishing me?" kind.)

We went to the doctor, and he gave what to me seemed like a preposterous prescription straight out of a Betty Crocker cookbook: *an oatmeal bath*.

I was somewhere between disgusted and horrified.

"An oatmeal bath?" I said indignantly. "That's not medicine, that's breakfast!" I was resolute. No oatmeal was going near my body unless it came with brown sugar and a spoon.

But two days later, I was rethinking everything. The pain and itching were unbearable. I felt like a human bee sting. In desperation, I approached my mother like a battered warrior asking for a truce. "OK," I said meekly. "I'm ready for the bath."

She didn't say "I told you so"—at least not until the second or third retelling. She drew the bath and poured in the oats, and I climbed in, defeated. But my drama wasn't over.

My mom was about to leave for a business trip. Her bags were packed, her ride to Newark Airport was scheduled, and she was wearing her skirt suit. And there

I was, sitting in a warm tub of Quaker mush, giving her the plaintive eyes of a Dickensian orphan.

"Mom," I said, with all the melodrama a ten-year-old could muster, "if you leave me now, I will die."

She stared at me. Hard. Then she left the room.

I thought that was it. She was going to the airport. I was going to perish alone in a tub of breakfast food.

But then . . . she came back. Out of her business attire, now in sweats. She had canceled her business trip, meetings and all. She sat down next to the tub.

She smiled gently and said, simply, "I'll stay."

I was overreacting, I was being needy and over the top, and she knew it. She knew that the chicken pox might end up being one of the easier things I would experience in my life, that I would certainly have worse days than sitting in an oatmeal bath. But she stayed with me. She saw me. And amid all my discomfort, I felt deeply loved.

This feels like an important spot to note that the only reason my mom was able to stay with me that day is because she had a job that let her. Her company had a generous family leave policy, and she didn't have to lose a paycheck to care for me. We had good healthcare—so when the school nurse called to say I likely had chicken pox, my mom could take me to the doctor without worrying about whether we could afford it.

But somehow as I write this today, over four decades later, most parents in our country still don't have paid family leave. They can't take time off without risking their paycheck. Despite the progress we have made, the cost of healthcare is still the number one reason families in this country have to declare bankruptcy.[6] My family didn't have to choose between making a mortgage payment and affording medicine. We didn't have to worry about missing a car payment in order to pay for a visit to the pediatrician. What my family had then still isn't normal today. It is a luxury and a privilege. And it shouldn't be. Not in the United States of America.

In his 1964 acceptance speech for the Nobel Prize, Martin Luther King Jr. said, "I have the audacity to believe that people everywhere can have three meals a day for their bodies, education and culture for their minds, and dignity, equality, and freedom for their spirits."[7] When it comes to our public policy, we must dare to have those kinds of audacious dreams today, where the United States of America leads the world in its GDP, world-class research universities, pioneering advanced technologies, and scientific breakthroughs—*and* in elevating human dignity, health, and well-being for its citizens. A nation with jobs that pay well, safe neighborhoods that nurture families, and education systems that launch children to greater heights of human achievement, where we have not only a moonshot to cure diseases like cancer, Alzheimer's, and Parkinson's but a moonshot to tackle the exploding mental health crisis. A nation where every parent can care for a newborn or sick child without losing their job; where we have affordable childcare so parents can work without losing half their paycheck to day care; where we have universal pre-K, because approximately 90 percent of childhood brain development happens before the age of five; and where we have living wages for caregivers, because the people we trust with our loved ones shouldn't be scraping by.[8]

What is our big, bold, impossible vision? We're the wealthiest nation on earth, the nation that mapped the human genome, that defied gravity and ascended to the moon, that defeated tyranny and won two world wars. We have done impossible things before. We should act like it now.

This is a generational moment. The torch is passing and a new generation of leaders must rise—not simply to inherit power but to renew purpose. And with a new generation must come a new vision that meets the moment with imagination and courage.

We can build an America that doesn't shrink from its challenges but rises to them; that doesn't turn against itself but toward one another. An America that once again believes in the promise that we can do big, bold, impossible things—together.

I am determined to fight for policies that confront our most urgent crises and summon the best of who we are: our innovation, our grit, our compassion, and our courage.

But this book is not about one leader's vision. It is

about our vision. It is a call for something deeper. It is an invitation to every reader to ask, What is my vision, for myself, for my family, for my community, and for my country that is rooted in our nation's most cherished values? Such a vision must begin with how we see one another, how we show up for one another, and how we treat one another.

* * *

THERE IS an old prayer that says, *God, grant me at least one friend who truly knows me and is still my friend anyway.*

For me, one of those friends is Kevin Batts. Kevin is a former Newark Police Department detective and US Army reservist who was born in Newark, New Jersey, and grew up in the Christopher Columbus Homes public housing projects. He was part of my security detail when I was mayor of Newark and is now a key member of my team in the Senate. Kevin and I have spent literally thousands of hours together over the better part of two decades, traveling the nation from museums like the Lorraine Motel to national parks like Yellowstone. Most often, our time together is spent in a car driving around New Jersey.

During that time, Kevin has developed an uncanny ability to read my mind. He knows when to blast gospel music to lift my spirit or dispel some stress. He knows when to give me just the right feedback or insight about my work. He knows when I need to be challenged or pushed or have my ego checked. Tragically, Kevin is a Dallas Cowboys fan, a particularly acute betrayal for a man who grew up in Giants territory. Nobody's perfect. During football season, our car can become a hostile place. But the rest of the time, it is a sanctuary for me and Kevin, a humble and wise man who has made me a better version of myself.

A few years back, we were driving a few blocks from my home in Newark, when Kevin, with his near-psychic powers, locked eyes with me in the rearview mirror and immediately knew what to do. Without words, judgments, or even a look of pity, he turned into the McDonald's drive-through. Without hesitation, I ordered two large fries. I paid at the window and clutched the bag of fries to my chest. I must have looked like Gollum from *The Lord of the Rings*; I might as well have been muttering "My precious, my precious . . ."

On the way out, I saw a man leaning over a trash container at the end of the drive-through. Kevin saw him too. He stopped the car, and I called out my window, "Hey, man, you all right?" He waved me off without even turning to look at me.

I realized my tone wasn't quite right. It was too cavalier and lacked respect. I tried again. "Sir, anything I can do to be helpful?"

He turned around, looked at me, studied me for a moment, and then said, "I am hungry."

Clearly, I didn't need two large fries. And as a person of faith, I can't remember exactly where, but I know Jesus said something like, "If you have two McDonald's french fries and your neighbor has none . . . give your neighbor one." Perhaps it was the Sermon on the McMount.*

I reached into the bag, pulled out half of my treasure, and handed it to him.

He seemed happy. I felt good about myself. Then the man said, "Hey, you wouldn't have any socks, would you?"

I knew immediately why he was asking. Socks can be one of the most requested items for people experiencing homelessness. I didn't carry extra socks in my car. I felt bad, but I told him I didn't have any.

He seemed a little disappointed, but he stepped back from the car and nodded as he raised the fries in appreciation. I smiled and nodded back and then turned forward, expecting Kevin to drive; soon I would be home on my couch, resting from a long day and watching some mindless TV while eating my hot, crispy treasure.

But Kevin didn't drive. He was too busy being true to himself.

* Sorry.

I looked at him a little harder into the rearview mirror, trying to convey *I want to go home* telepathically, but Kevin ignored my mental message. He put the car in park. He kicked off his shoes, reached down, and took the socks he was wearing off his feet. He folded them with care and respectfully handed them through the window to the man. The man received them and beamed with gratitude.

I was three blocks from my house, where I have a drawer full of socks. I saw the man in front of me that day, but I didn't have the moral vision to take off my socks and give them to a man who had humbled himself enough to ask for them. Kevin did.

I have learned in life that we must infuse moral vision into the big things we pursue—the big idea, the big policy, the big speech, standing up proudly for what is right.

But more often, the most important thing we can do is to put our moral vision into seemingly small, everyday moments—moments that need more kindness, decency, or love. Perhaps that is how we can start to make the big changes our society needs more possible—more inevitable, even.

Over the course of this book, I have argued that our nation urgently needs more of us to commit to, elevate, and celebrate our shared values—to live our virtues now as much as ever.

Our country needs each of us, every day, to recognize our agency and remember our power, to be courageously vulnerable, especially when it's hardest to be, and to be patriots who don't just love our nation, but also love our fellow Americans.

Our country needs us to tell the truth about who we are and who we have been, and it needs us to be more willing to embrace the humility that creates space for possibility. It needs us to be bridge builders who repair and renew community; to be creative artists of activism, bringing imagination to our challenges, large and small; and to persevere in the face of daunting odds.

Our country needs us to extend grace—to one another and to ourselves. And it needs us to carry an expansive vision for our shared future—and for how we see one another.

Our country needs each of us, every day, to ***stand.***

And on some days, our country just needs us to take off our socks.

Acknowledgments

This is a book about virtue, made possible only by the extraordinary virtues of the community of people who supported, encouraged, and sustained me through the—often difficult, at times spirit-crushing, yet always affirming—process of bringing it to completion.

Quite simply, this book would not exist as you see it without Marissa Brogger—my former speechwriter and forever friend. Her discipline, deep research, meticulous attention to detail, and profoundly steadfast work ethic are, in great part, responsible for this book's completion.

But Marissa was far more than an editor or collaborator; she was also my coach, my therapist, and my fiercest constructive critic. She challenged me at every turn, reined in my worst writing instincts, and, I must admit, was right roughly 90 percent of the time when we disagreed (a fact she will no doubt underline when she reads this).

And the reader should thank her as well—for she waged a tireless campaign against my awesome affection for alliteration, always arguing for its absence. So let me end by saying this: If this book stands as a worthy offering, it is because of Marissa Brogger's creative collaboration, witty writing, fastidious fact-finding, and fabulously fortifying friendship.

Jennifer Joel and Esther Newberg, my longtime agents and dear friends, were indispensable in launching the idea of this book. All along the way, they offered encouragement, guidance, and just the right amount of pressure to see it through. You are both forces of nature, and I am deeply grateful—for your wisdom, for your persistence, and for always being in my corner.

Tim Bartlett at St. Martin's Press believed in this book before I even knew I was going to write it. His early faith in the project helped get it off the ground, and his diligence—and occasional tough love—kept it moving toward completion. Tim's editorial insight was invaluable, particularly in shaping the chapters Vulnerability, Humility, and Community—you encouraged me to humble myself and be more vulnerable in my writing. I am also grateful for the excellent edits and steady stream of sharp suggestions from Kevin Reilly, who brought clarity to my ideas and strengthened every chapter.

I'm also profoundly thankful to the entire team at St. Martin's Press who brought this book to life: Olga Grlic, Lizz Blaise, Martin Quinn, Tracey Guest, Paul Hochman, Gabrielle Gantz, Susannah Noel, Chris Leonowicz, Allison Gudenau, Lauren Riebs, Laura Clark,

Meryl Levavi, Soleil Paz, Elishia Merricks, Emily Dyer, and Drew Kilman. Your expertise, energy, and care made this book far better than I could have made it alone.

Ben Kalin undertook the arduous and time-consuming work of fact-checking this book with precision, conscientiousness, and skill. I am deeply grateful for the many nights and weekends he spent patiently poring over multiple drafts—diving deep into history, testing my claims, and refining my words. His quiet rigor and intellectual generosity were an anchor throughout this process.

This book was born from people who had the courage to share their stories when it was most difficult to do so. I am deeply grateful to my constituents, the people of the great state of New Jersey—and to people across the country—who reached out with letters, phone calls, and messages that inspired, challenged, and sustained me over the past year.

I am also profoundly thankful to the community of people whose time, energy, and heart are reflected in these pages through their interviews. I am especially grateful to Wanda Williams-Bailey for her generous letter and for taking the time to share more about her family's story with me. I am likewise grateful to Neil deGrasse Tyson, who shared his sense of awe at the universe—and his moving words honoring the beautiful life of Annaliese Backner. I am thankful, too, to have gotten to know the extraordinary activist Jennifer Keelan-Chaffins and her mother Cynthia Keelan, who graciously shared their inspiring story. Judge

Esther Salas has moved me again and again through her indomitable grace and her love for her son, Daniel Anderl. It was an honor to tell part of her and Mark Anderl's story and to highlight their urgent, hope-filled work.

Kevin Batts embodies what it means to be both a patriot and a public servant—through his service in the United States Army Reserves, his years as a Newark Police Department detective, and now as a member of my Senate staff. But most of all, he embodies patriotism through the way he loves his neighbor. Having Kevin as a friend is a blessing beyond expression, and sharing a small part of what he has taught me is a joy. Thank you, Kevin, for allowing me to include some of your story. For decades now, I have been grateful to have you—often literally—by my side (even though you are a Dallas Cowboys fan).

I am profoundly fortunate to be surrounded by an extraordinary community of people who supported me throughout the writing of this book, and whose feedback made it stronger. Chad Maisel has been a constant source of insight, creativity, and partnership—offering ideas and contributions that approach even the most intractable policy challenges with imagination and depth. I am grateful to him.

I am sustained, encouraged, and uplifted by a team of remarkable people. I am especially thankful to Veronica Duron—who leads our team and drives my work with nurturing love and fierce compassion and is a Reiki master, tarot card reader, and baby-delivering doula, which make her the most unique Senate chief of staff in history and someone I adore, even though she has surrounded my desk with crystals I don't understand; Sarah Rojas—whose leadership, boundless heart, endless empathy, and tough but invaluable counsel make me and my work extraordinarily better; Hanna Mori—my longtime friend who leads our Jersey team and embodies the best of New Jersey in her ethics and the best of America in her excellence in execution; Matt Klapper—whose longtime friendship, counsel, and support are indispensable in my work and my life; Matt might indeed be a real-life superhero and showed me the power of marrying someone better than yourself; Modia Butler—I have soared in life because he was once my chief of staff in Newark; his guidance, friendship, and wisdom continue to be some of my life's greatest gifts; Adam Silverstein—whose strategic insights, rock-solid character, and invaluable leadership empower me in my mission of service; Mike Frosolone—whose noble heart, Margaritaville spirit, and strategic political excellence sharpen my vision and advance my work and make my world much more joyous; Leah Hill—who expertly leads and empowers our legislative team to do great things and drives my policy priorities and so many of our successes; she is a goddess of grace and goodness;

Adam Zipkin—whose moral magnitude and minutiae mastery have motivated me for three decades; his example of virtue-grounded leadership challenges me to be better; David Bergstein—who skillfully leads my communications strategy and sharpens and drives my messaging and is making me better in so many ways; Jeff Giertz—a true man of honor, whose longtime leadership and friendship on my team elevate our work and set an example of the impact of possessing a strong character and constant kindness; Ian Gray—whose freaking brilliant counsel and impressive creativity have strengthened my work and expanded my vision and sense of what is possible; Mitchell Smith—a prince of a human being and an increasingly vital part of my team and our mission; and Mather Martin—who has been by my side for many years (though she is decades younger than me) as a cherished advisor, an invaluable truth-telling friend, and a truly sagacious old soul.

I am endlessly thankful to Stefan Suric, Jordan Rosner, and Rob Kelly for everything they do to keep me moving—quite literally making sure the trains between Washington, DC, and New Jersey run on time. Their willingness to go way above and beyond in supporting me empowers my work and strengthens my purpose. Thank you to my friend Joanna Spilker for your extraordinary attention to detail and generous feedback; to my friend Lane Bodian for your steadfast support; and to Jacquelyn Lopez, Avery Woodard, and Kate Keane at Elias Law Group for their essential legal guidance.

I am grateful as well to the wider circle of people whose words and deeds helped shape and inspire this book: Kayanna Spooner, Joseph Peters, Chris Peters, Bryan Stevenson, Ron Finley, Senator Bill Bradley, Senator Raphael Warnock, former Vice President Kamala Harris, and Associate Justice Ketanji Brown Jackson.

I owe a deep debt of gratitude to those whose time on earth has ended but whose presence endures in my life and in these pages: Lee Porter, Arthur Lessman, Marty Friedman, Congressman John Lewis, Senator John McCain, Wazn Miller, Ms. Virginia Jones, and Ms. Jean Wright. And, of course, to my family, whose stories, faith, and wisdom fill this book—my grandmother Adeline Jordan, my grandfather Limuary Jordan, and my father, Cary Booker. I also want to thank my two brothers, Cary Booker and John Taylor, who show up for me in every challenge and every dream—and who make me a better human being.

Many other leaders, authors, historians, scholars, and journalists—past and present—influenced my thinking through their own extraordinary work. I encourage readers to explore the notes section of this book to learn more about their contributions.

Finally, I want to acknowledge and thank Alexis Lewis. During the writing of this book, she went from my girlfriend, to us moving in together, to my fiancée. In fact, I used this very book to throw her off the trail that I was planning to propose. I confess, I lied to her: I told her I couldn't even think about getting engaged until the book was finished. It worked—she was surprised (shocked, actually) when I proposed before the final chapters were complete.

Throughout this journey, Alexis has been my indispensable counsel and my constant source of strength—the one who renewed, restored, and recharged my spirit again and again. Thank you, My Love, for making space for this work without complaint—even on our engagement weekend—and for inspiring me to pour the best of my heart into these pages. I love you. And I pray that as you read these words, you are indeed Alexis L. Booker.

NOTES

Introduction

1. Jas. M. Guthrie, *Camp-Fires of the Afro-American; or, The Colored Man as a Patriot* (Afro-American Pub. Co., 1899), 270.

1. Agency

1. Lana Weinstein, "Repent, Repair, Renew," Reform Judaism (blog), August 31, 2023.
2. Elbert L. Watson, "Edmund Pettus," *Encyclopedia of Alabama*, November 9, 2010.
3. Joshua Lewis, "Civil Rights Activists Mark 40 Years Since 'Bloody Sunday,'" *VOA*, October 30, 2009, https://www.voanews.com/a/a-13-2005-03-04-voa53/396308.html.
4. Gene Roberts and Hank Klibanoff, *The Race Beat: The Press, the Civil Rights Struggle, and the Awakening of a Nation* (Vintage Books, 2006), 386.
5. Roberts and Klibanoff, *The Race Beat*, 387–388.
6. Lyndon B. Johnson, "Special Message to the Congress: The American Promise," March 15, 1965, American Presidency Project, accessed October 19, 2025, https://www.lbjlibrary.org/object/text/special-message-congress-american-promise-03-15-1965.
7. "Jackson, Jimmie Lee," Martin Luther King, Jr. Research and

Education Institute, Stanford University, accessed October 19, 2025, https://kinginstitute.stanford.edu/jackson-jimmie-lee.

8. Nick Kotz, *Judgement Days: Lyndon Baines Johnson, Martin Luther King, Jr., and the Laws That Changed America* (Houghton Mifflin, 2005), 276.
9. Johann Christoph Arnold, "Selma, 1965: The Unforgettable Funeral of Jimmie Lee Jackson," *Plough*, January 15, 2015, https://www.plough.com/en/topics/justice/social-justice/selma-1965-jimmie-lee-jacksons-funeral; A. Fitts III, "Good Samaritan Hospital and Nursing Home, Inc., Selma, Al. Hospital-Affiliated Clinics Meet Health Needs of Rural Poor," *Hospital Progress* 62, no. 2 (1981): 40–41.
10. Martin Luther King, Jr., "Eulogy for Jimmie Lee Jackson," March 3, 1965, Martin Luther King, Jr. Research and Education Institute, Stanford University, accessed October 19, 2025, https://kinginstitute.stanford.edu/jackson-jimmie-lee.
11. Cory Booker, *United: Thoughts on Finding Common Ground and Advancing the Common Good* (Ballantine Books, 2016), 16–17.
12. Monsy Alvarado, "Meet North Jersey's 91-Year-Old Fair Housing Champion," *Bergen Record*, August 13, 2018, https://www.northjersey.com/story/news/new-jersey/2018/08/13/meet-north-jerseys-91-year-old-fair-housing-champion/868178002/.
13. Booker, *United*, 19–20.
14. Janell Ross, "Body of Rep. John Lewis Crosses Bridge Where, at 25, He Thought He Would Be Killed," NBC News, July 26, 2020.

2. Vulnerability

1. Maya Goldman, "Musk's Team Accesses Medicare, Medicaid Records," *Axios*, February 6, 2025, https://www.axios.com/2025/02/06/elon-musk-doge-health-data-cms.
2. Julie Carter, "Trump Administration and Elon Musk's DOGE

Closing Social Security Offices, Harming Access to Services," Medicare Rights Center, March 13, 2025, https://www.medicarerights.org/medicare-watch/2025/03/13/trump-administration-and-elon-musks-doge-closing-social-security-offices-harming-access-to-services.

3. "Howard Lutnick | All-In DC," *All-In Podcast*, March 20, 2025, YouTube, https://www.youtube.com/watch?v=182ckTL2KBA&t=23s.
4. Brenda Flanagan, "Frustrations Mount for NJ Beneficiaries of Social Security," *NJ Spotlight News*, March 28, 2025, https://www.njspotlightnews.org/video/frustrations-mount-for-nj-beneficiaries-of-social-security/.
5. David E. Rosenbaum, "Filibuster Foes Win the Key Test and Limit Debate," *New York Times*, March 6, 1975, https://www.nytimes.com/1975/03/06/archives/filibuster-foes-win-the-key-test-and-limit-debate.html.
6. Jonathan Weisman, "Senator Persists Battling Health Law, Irking Even Many in His Own Party," *New York Times*, September 24, 2013, https://www.nytimes.com/2013/09/25/us/politics/senate-democratic-leader-sets-stage-for-budget-showdown.html.
7. James 5:16.
8. Brené Brown, *Daring Greatly: How the Courage to Be Vulnerable Transforms the Way We Live, Love, Parent, and Lead* (Avery, 2012), 37.
9. Al Swanson, "Commentary: Strom's Dark Secret," UPI, December 17, 2003, https://www.upi.com/Defense-News/2003/12/17/Commentary-Stroms-dark-secret/61631071701388/.

3. Patriotism

1. Guthrie, *Camp-Fires of the Afro-American*, 313.
2. Guthrie, *Camp-Fires*.
3. Gerald S. Henig, "Meet the Unstoppable Mr. Smalls," *Navy Times*, February 12, 2019, https://www.navytimes.com/news/your-navy/2019/02/12/meet-the-unstoppable-mr-smalls/.

4. Cate Lineberry, *Be Free or Die: The Amazing Story of Robert Smalls' Escape from Slavery to Union Hero* (St. Martin's Press, 2017), 11–12, 21.
5. Andrew Billingsley, *Yearning to Breathe Free: Robert Smalls of South Carolina and His Families* (University of South Carolina Press, 2021), 1, 55–56.
6. United States House of Representatives Report. No. 47–1962 (February 19, 1883), 2. The Congressional report had the name of the captain misspelled; his correct name was Captain Charles J. Relyea.
7. Lineberry, *Be Free or Die*, 23.
8. Billingsley, *Yearning*, 58.
9. Lineberry, *Be Free or Die*, 26–27.
10. Guthrie, *Camp-Fires*, 313.
11. Lineberry, *Be Free or Die*, 73.
12. Billingsley, *Yearning*, 63, 69–70.
13. Henig, "Meet the Unstoppable Mr. Smalls."
14. Billingsley, *Yearning*, 85.
15. "Robert Smalls," National Park Service, accessed October 19, 2025, https://www.nps.gov/people/robert-smalls.htm.
16. Billingsley, *Yearning*, 107.
17. Billingsley, *Yearning*, 162.
18. Lineberry, *Be Free or Die*, 229.
19. Andrew Lapin, host, *Radioactive: The Father Coughlin Story*, podcast, episode 6, "Social Justice," Tablet Studios, PBS, March 9, 2022, https://www.pbs.org/wnet/exploring-hate/2022/03/09/ep-6-social-justice.
20. Beverly Gage, "How the Red Scare Reshaped American Politics," *The New Yorker*, March 10, 2025, https://www.newyorker.com/magazine/2025/03/17/red-scare-clay-risen-book-review.
21. James Baldwin, *Notes of a Native Son* (Beacon Press, 1955), 9.
22. Marisa Mathias, "Susan B. Anthony," National Women's History Museum, accessed October 19, 2025, https://www.womenshistory.org/education-resources/biographies/susan-b-anthony.

23. "Mary Ann Shadd Cary," National Park Service, accessed October 19, 2025, https://www.nps.gov/people/mary-ann-shadd-cary.htm; "Five You Should Know: African American Suffragists," National Museum of African American History & Culture, accessed October 19, 2025, https://nmaahc.si.edu/explore/stories/five-you-should-know-african-american-suffragists.
24. Alan Ramirez, "American Indian Veterans Have Highest Record of Military Service," National Indian Council on Aging, November 8, 2019, https://www.nicoa.org/american-indian-veterans-have-highest-record-of-military-service/.
25. A. J. Orlikoff, "Daniel K. Inouye," National Museum of the United States Army, accessed October 19, 2025, https://www.thenmusa.org/biographies/daniel-k-inouye/.
26. John S. McCain, "John McCain, Prisoner of War: A First-Person Account," *U.S. News & World Report*, January 28, 2008.
27. "The Facts About John McCain," McCain Institute, March 20, 2019, https://www.mccaininstitute.org/resources/blog/the-facts-about-john-mccain/.
28. "Capt. John McCain's Speech," *WAFB9*, October 11, 2001, https://www.wafb.com/story/505192/capt-john-mccains-speech/.
29. Dylan Scott, "I'll Never Forget Watching John McCain Vote Down Obamacare Repeal," *Vox*, August 27, 2018, https://www.vox.com/policy-and-politics/2018/8/25/17782664/john-mccain-legacy-obamacare-repeal-thumbs-down.
30. Jessica Estepa, "Watch Sen. John McCain's Speech About Returning to Regular Order," *USA Today*, August 30, 2018, https://www.usatoday.com/story/news/politics/onpolitics/2018/08/30/john-mccain-senate-speech-regular-order-remarks/1145189002/.
31. Bill Bradley, *Rolling Along: An American Story*, HBO Max, February 1, 2024.
32. Guthrie, *Camp-Fires*, 313.
33. Stephen R. Wise and Lawrence S. Rowland, *Rebellion, Reconstruction, and Redemption, 1861–1893: The History of Beaufort*

County, South Carolina (University of South Carolina Press, 2015), 489.

34. Wise and Rowland, *Rebellion*, 489.
35. Lineberry, *Be Free or Die*, 225.

4. Truth

1. Malia Rulon Herman, "Cory Booker Sworn into U.S. Senate," *USA Today*, October 31, 2013, https://www.usatoday.com/story/news/politics/2013/10/31/booker-sworn-into-office/3324501/.
2. Benjamin Justesen, "George Henry White: A Sketch," NCPedia, State Library of NC, 2013, https://www.ncpedia.org/anchor/george-henry-white.
3. Chris Franklin, "Effort Underway to Name N.J. Post Office After Congressman Who Helped Displaced Black Residents," NJ.com, February 16, 2023, https://www.nj.com/cape-may-county/2020/07/effort-underway-to-name-nj-post-office-after-congressman-who-helped-displaced-black-residents.html.
4. "Reconstructing Citizenship," National Museum of African American History & Culture, accessed October 17, 2025, https://nmaahc.si.edu/explore/exhibitions/reconstruction/citizenship.
5. "Reconstruction in America: Racial Violence After the Civil War, 1865–1876," Equal Justice Initiative, 2020, https://eji.org/report/reconstruction-in-america/.
6. "Daniel L. Russell 1845–1908 (D-92)," North Carolina Department of Natural Resources, December 11, 2023, https://www.dncr.nc.gov/blog/2023/12/11/daniel-l-russell-1845-1908-d-92.
7. Jan Davidson, "When White Supremacists Overthrew a Government," PBS, *American Experience*, October 23, 2024, https://www.pbs.org/wgbh/americanexperience/features/when-white-supremacists-overthrew-government/.
8. DeNeen L. Brown, "Majority-Black Wilmington, N.C., Fell to White Mob's Coup 125 Years Ago," *The Washington Post*, November 10, 2023, https://www.washingtonpost.com/history/2023/11/10/wilmington-massacre-150-anniversary/.

9. W.J. Martin, "Rioting in Wilmington," *Charlotte Daily Observer*, November 10, 1898.
10. "Senate Stories | Rebecca Felton and One Hundred Years of Women Senators," United States Senate, November 21, 2022, https://www.senate.gov/artandhistory/senate-stories/rebecca-felton-and-one-hundred-years-of-women-senators.htm.
11. "Alexander Manly ca. 1870–1890," 1898 Election in North Carolina, UNC Libraries, accessed October 19, 2025, https://exhibits.lib.unc.edu/exhibits/show/1898/newbios/manly.
12. J. Allen Kirk, *A Statement of Facts Concerning the Bloody Riot in Wilmington, N.C. of Interest to Every Citizen of the United States* (Forgotten Books, 2018), 9–12, https://www.ncpedia.org/anchor/primary-source-j-allen-kirk.
13. Davidson, "When White Supremacists."
14. Michael Hill and LeRae Umfleet, "Manly, Alex," NCpedia, 2010, revised by SLNC Government & Heritage Library, 2023, https://www.ncpedia.org/biography/manly-alex.
15. Hill and Umfleet, "Manly, Alex."
16. "American Coup: Wilmington 1898," PBS, *American Experience*, November 12, 2024, https://www.pbs.org/wgbh/americanexperience/films/american-coup-wilmington-1898/#transcript.
17. "North Carolina Votes to Disenfranchise Black Residents: On This Day—Aug. 02, 1900," A History of Racial Injustice, Equal Justice Initiative, https://calendar.eji.org/racial-injustice/aug/2.
18. "George Henry White," National Museum of African American History & Culture, accessed October 19, 2025, https://www.searchablemuseum.com/george-henry-white/.
19. "Anti-Lynching Petition," February 21, 1900, History, Art & Archives, United States House of Representatives, https://history.house.gov/Records-and-Research/Listing/pm_031/.
20. "Defense of the Negro Race—Charges Answered. Speech of Hon. George H. White, of North Carolina, in the House of

Representatives, January 29, 1901," Civil War Era NC, North Carolina State University, accessed October 19, 2025, https://cwnc.omeka.chass.ncsu.edu/items/show/417.

21. Marty Roney, "EJI's Lynching Memorial: If Not in Montgomery, Then Where?," *Montgomery Advertiser*, April 19, 2018, https://www.montgomeryadvertiser.com/story/news/2018/04/19/ejis-lynching-memorial-if-not-montgomery-then-where/522568002/.
22. "Dedication of the National Memorial for Peace and Justice," Equal Justice Initiative, October 29, 2018, YouTube, 7:00, https://www.youtube.com/watch?v=1pUNPAsI6zc.
23. Terry Gross, "'Just Mercy' Attorney Asks U.S. to Reckon with Its Racist Past and Present," *Fresh Air*, NPR, January 20, 2020, https://www.npr.org/transcripts/796234496.
24. Gross, "'Just Mercy' Attorney."
25. John Chrastka, Marilyn Jackson, and Celina Stewart, "The Trump Administration Is Not Just Erasing History, They're Rewriting the Future and Attacking Democracy," *Newsweek*, April 18, 2025, https://www.newsweek.com/trump-administration-not-just-erasing-history-theyre-rewriting-future-attacking-democracy-2061128.
26. Chris Hayes, *The Sirens' Call: How Attention Became the World's Most Endangered Resource* (Penguin Press, 2025), 205.
27. Hayes, *Sirens' Call*, 210.
28. "Justice Department Leads Efforts Among Federal, International, and Private Sector Partners to Disrupt Covert Russian Government-Operated Social Media Bot Farm," US Department of Justice, July 9, 2024, https://www.justice.gov/archives/opa/pr/justice-department-leads-efforts-among-federal-international-and-private-sector-partners.
29. Becky Little, "When Ida B. Wells Took on Lynching, Threats Forced Her to Leave Memphis," History.com, August 2, 2018, https://www.history.com/articles/ida-b-wells-lynching-memphis-chicago.

30. “A Lecture,” an advertisement for one of Wells’s speeches, *Washington Bee*, October 22, 1892.
31. Aaron Blake, “African Americans in Congress by the Numbers,” *The Washington Post*, August 28, 2013, https://www.washingtonpost.com/news/the-fix/wp/2013/08/28/african-americans-in-congress-by-the-numbers/; *Black Americans in Congress 1870–2022* (Office of the Historian and Office of the Clerk, United States House of Representatives, 2023), https://www.govinfo.gov/content/pkg/GPO-CDOC-118hdoc16/pdf/GPO-CDOC-118hdoc16.pdf.
32. George H. White, “Farewell Address to Congress,” January 29, 1901.
33. Mamie Till-Mobley and Christopher Benson, *Death of Innocence: The Story of the Hate Crime That Changed America* (Random House, 2003), xxiii.

5. Humility

1. CBS News, *Sunday Morning*, April 30, 2017.
2. Judge Learned Hand, “The Spirit of Liberty” speech, May 21, 1944.
3. Abraham Lincoln, “Second Inaugural Address, March 4, 1865,” https://housedivided.dickinson.edu/sites/lincoln/second-inaugural-address-march-4–1865/.
4. Frederick Douglass, *Life and Times of Frederick Douglass* (Park Publishing, 1881), 443–444.
5. Douglass, *Life and Times*, 443.
6. Douglass, *Life and Times*, 444–445.
7. Waldo E. Martin Jr., “Frederick Douglass: Humanist as Race Leader,” in *Black Leaders of the Nineteenth Century*, ed. Leon Litwack and August Meier (University of Illinois Press, 1988), 76.
8. Sarah Fling, “Frederick Douglass and Abraham Lincoln,” White House Historical Association, December 4, 2019, https:

//www.whitehousehistory.org/frederick-douglass-and-abraham-lincoln.

9. Elsie Freeman, Wynell Burroughs Schamel, and Jean West, "The Fight for Equal Rights: A Recruiting Poster for Black Soldiers in the Civil War," *Social Education* 56, no. 2 (1992): 118–120.
10. Douglass, *Life and Times*, 445.
11. Kirk Savage, "Who Owns a Monument?," PBS, *American Experience*, February 5, 2021, https://www.pbs.org/wgbh/americanexperience/features/voice-freedom-who-owns-monument/.
12. John Stauffer, *Giants: The Parallel Lives of Frederick Douglass and Abraham Lincoln* (Twelve, 2008), 305.
13. Douglass, *Life and Times*, 587.
14. Douglass, *Life and Times*, 587–588.
15. Douglass, *Life and Times*, 593–594.
16. Dennis Whitcomb, Heather Battaly, Jason Baehr, and Daniel Howard-Snyder, "The Puzzle of Humility and Disparity," in *The Routledge Handbook of Philosophy of Humility*, ed. M. Alfano, M. P. Lynch, and A. Tanesini (Routledge, 2021), 72–83, https://digitalcommons.lmu.edu/cgi/viewcontent.cgi?article=1298&context=phil_fac.
17. Whitcomb et al., "The Puzzle"; Megan Phelps-Roper, "I Grew Up in the Westboro Baptist Church. Here's Why I Left," TED Talk, February 2017, https://ed.ted.com/lessons/i-grew-up-in-the-westboro-baptist-church-here-s-why-i-left-megan-phelps-roper.

6. Community

1. Booker, *United*, 50.
2. Robert Putnam, *Bowling Alone: The Collapse and Revival of American Community* (Simon & Schuster, 2000), 27.
3. *Our Epidemic of Loneliness and Isolation: The U.S. Surgeon General's*

Advisory on the Healing Effects of Social Connection and Community (Office of the Surgeon General, 2023), 4, https://www.hhs.gov/sites/default/files/surgeon-general-social-connection-advisory.pdf.

4. John T. Cacioppo and William Patrick, *Loneliness: Human Nature and the Need for Social Connection* (W.W. Norton, 2008), 34.
5. *Our Epidemic of Loneliness and Isolation*, 4.
6. Cacioppo and Patrick, *Loneliness*, 223.
7. Cacioppo and Patrick, *Loneliness*, 7.
8. Cacioppo and Patrick, *Loneliness*, 173.
9. David Brooks, "The Relationalist Manifesto," The Aspen Institute, May 2025, https://www.aspeninstitute.org/wp-content/uploads/2025/05/Weave-Relationalist-Manifesto.pdf.
10. Aditi Shrikant, "Brené Brown on the No. 1 Way to Combat Loneliness: 'It Was One of the Best Things That Ever Happened to Me,'" CNBC, April 9, 2024.
11. Steve Levitsky and Daniel Ziblatt, *How Democracies Die* (Crown, 2018), vii.
12. Becca Rashid and Arthur C. Brooks, "How to Know You're Lonely," *The Atlantic*, October 12, 2021, https://www.theatlantic.com/podcasts/archive/2021/10/howto-friendship-loneliness-arthurbrooks-vivekmurthy-happiness/620281/.
13. Vivek H. Murthy, *Together: The Healing Power of Human Connection in a Sometimes Lonely World* (Harper Wave, 2020), 89.
14. Patrick McGorry, Hasini Gunasiri, Cristina Mei, Simon Rice, and Caroline X. Gao, "The Youth Mental Health Crisis: Analysis and Solutions," *Frontiers in Psychiatry* 15, no. 2024 (January 20, 2025): 4.
15. "The Three Biggest Mental Health Centers in America Are Jails," WLNS, February 25, 2020, https://www.wlns.com/news/national/the-three-biggest-mental-health-centers-in-america-are-jails/.
16. Tyler D. Harvey, Susan H. Busch, Hsiu-Ju Lin, Jenerius A.

Aminawung, Lisa Puglisi, Shira Shavit, et al., "Cost Savings of a Primary Care Program for Individuals Recently Released from Prison: A Propensity-Matched Study," *BMC Health Services Research* 22, no. 585 (2002), https://bmchealthservres.biomedcentral.com/articles/10.1186/s12913-022-07985-5.

17. Josh Katz, "Short Answers to Hard Questions About the Opioid Crisis," *New York Times,* August 10, 2017, https://www.nytimes.com/interactive/2017/08/03/upshot/opioid-drug-overdose-epidemic.html.
18. Dallin Judd, Connor R. King, and Curtis Galke, "The Opioid Epidemic: A Review of the Contributing Factors, Negative Consequences, and Best Practices," *Cureus* 15, no. 7 (2023), https://pmc.ncbi.nlm.nih.gov/articles/PMC10410480/.
19. Damien Cave and Josh Benson, "Newark Candidate Runs Against His Own Fame," *New York Times*, May 4, 2006, https://www.nytimes.com/2006/05/04/nyregion/newark-candidate-runs-against-his-own-fame.html.
20. Barry Carter and Jeffrey C. Mays, "Newark Mayor and Rival Turn Youth Event into Shoving Match," *Star-Ledge*r, July 16, 2005.
21. Damien Cave, "With Shoves and Curses, Newark Political Rivalry Takes Ugly Turn," *New York Times*, July 16, 2005, https://www.nytimes.com/2005/07/16/nyregion/with-shoves-and-curses-newark-political-rivalry-takes-ugly-turn.html.
22. Scott Galloway, "Opinion: The Most Dangerous Person in the World: A Young Man Who's Broke and Alone," CNN, April 19, 2022, https://www.cnn.com/2022/04/19/opinions/masculinity-toxic-men-boys-education-galloway.
23. Kristina Rizga, "Cory Booker: The Art of Slashing Government," *Mother Jones*, November 13, 2010, https://www.motherjones.com/criminal-justice/2010/11/cory-booker-facebook-education/.
24. Cacioppo and Patrick, *Loneliness*, 236–237.
25. Murthy, *Together*, xv.

7. Creativity

1. Elie Wiesel, "The Perils of Indifference," East Room of the White House, April 12, 1999.
2. Doris Stevens, *Jailed for Freedom* (Liveright Publishing, 1920), 63–64.
3. Stevens, *Jailed*, 83.
4. Stevens, *Jailed*, 48.
5. Stevens, *Jailed*, 92.
6. Stevens, *Jailed*, 96.
7. Stevens, *Jailed*, 127.
8. "National Woman's Party Protests During World War I," National Park Service, accessed October 19, 2025, https://www.nps.gov/articles/national-womans-party-protests-world-war-i.htm.
9. Tina Cassidy, *Mr. President, How Long Must We Wait?: Alice Paul, Woodrow Wilson, and the Fight for the Right to Vote* (37 INK/Atria Books, 2019), 15; Stevens, *Jailed*, 94–95.
10. Stevens, *Jailed*, 142–146.
11. Stevens, *Jailed*, 201–202.
12. Stevens, *Jailed*, 184, 189.
13. Stevens, *Jailed*, 241.
14. Stevens, *Jailed*, 326.
15. "Moments in Disability History, Stories of Discrimination," ADA Legacy Project, Minnesota Department of Administration, August 1, 2014, https://mn.gov/mnddc/ada-legacy/ada-legacy-moment20.html.
16. *Equality of Opportunity: The Making of the Americans with Disabilities Act* (National Council on Disability, 1997), https://files.eric.ed.gov/fulltext/ED512697.pdf.
17. Rashed Mian, host, *InclusionHub*, podcast, episode 3, "The Capitol Crawl," August 25, 2022, https://www.inclusionhub.com/transcript/episode-3.
18. Steven A. Holmes, "Rights Bill for Disabled Is Sent to Bush," *New York Times*, July 14, 1990, https://www.nytimes.com/1990/07/14/us/rights-bill-for-disabled-is-sent-to-bush.html.

19. Arthur C. Brooks, "The Trouble with Zooming Forever," *The Atlantic*, July 14, 2022, https://www.theatlantic.com/family/archive/2022/07/how-to-fight-zoom-fatigue/670513/; Arthur C. Brooks, "Technology Can Make Your Relationships Shallower, *The Atlantic*, September 29, 2022, https://www.theatlantic.com/family/archive/2022/09/technology-happiness-communication-relationships/671586/.
20. Booker, *United*, 203, 208.
21. Ron Finley, "How Growing Carrots Almost Got Me Arrested," Thinking L.A., February 5, 2015, https://time.com/3697675/growing-carrots/.
22. Ron Finley, "A Guerilla Gardener in South Central LA," TED Talk, February 2013, https://www.ted.com/talks/ron_finley_a_guerrilla_gardener_in_south_central_la.
23. Albert Einstein, *Cosmic Religion* (Covici Friede, 1931), 97.

8. Perseverance

1. "Senate Chamber Desks," United States Senate, accessed October 19, 2025, https://www.senate.gov/art-artifacts/decorative-art/furniture/senate-chamber-desks/overview.htm.
2. "Senate Chamber Desks: Desk 3," United States Senate, accessed October 19, 2025, https://www.senate.gov/art-artifacts/decorative-art/furniture/senate-chamber-desks/desks/desk_3.htm.
3. Jennifer E. Manning, "Membership of the 119th Congress: A Profile," Congressional Research Service, August 4, 2025, https://www.congress.gov/crs-product/R48535.
4. "Women Senators," United States Senate, accessed October 19, 2025, https://www.senate.gov/senators/ListofWomenSenators.htm.
5. "About the Senate Chamber: Historical Overview," United States Senate, accessed October 19, 2025, https://www.senate.gov/about/historic-buildings-spaces/chamber/overview.htm.
6. R. I. Duffus, "Again the Palisades Are Threatened," *New York Times*, June 10, 1928, https://www.nytimes.com/1928/06/10

/archives/again-the-palisades-are-threatened-scarcely-have-the-hudson-river.html.

7. "Weehawken Dueling Grounds," HC Blog, Hudson County, New Jersey, October 11, 2023, https://www.visithudson.org/weehawken-dueling-grounds/.
8. Joan Verdon, "A Hike Back in Time to Era of Silent Film," *The Record*, March 5, 2012.
9. Peter Brannen, "Headstone for an Apocalypse," *New York Times*, August 16, 2013, https://www.nytimes.com/2013/08/17/opinion/headstone-for-an-apocalypse.html.
10. Terrence J. Blackburn, Paul E. Olsen, Samuel A. Bowring, Noah M. McLean, Dennis V. Kent, John Puffer, et al., "Zircon U-Pb Geochronology Links the End-Triassic Extinction with the Central Atlantic Magmatic Province," *Science*, March 21, 2023, https://www.science.org/doi/abs/10.1126/science.1234204; Mark Dziak, "Triassic-Jurassic Extinction Event," EBSCO, 2023, https://www.ebsco.com/research-starters/science/triassic-jurassic-extinction-event; Sebastian Modak, "Explore 200 Million Years of History in the Shadow of New York City," *National Geographic*, July 20, 2023, https://www.nationalgeographic.com/travel/article/new-york-palisades-massive-cliffs.
11. Jennifer Chu, "Huge and Widespread Volcanic Eruptions Triggered the End-Triassic Extinction," *MIT News*, March 21, 2013, https://news.mit.edu/2013/volcanic-eruptions-triggered-end-triassic-extinction-0321; Brannen, "Headstone for an Apocalypse."
12. David M. Rubenstein, *The American Story: Conversations with Master Historians* (Simon & Schuster, 2019), 8.
13. Rubenstein, *The American Story*, 8.
14. David McCullough, *1776* (Simon & Schuster, 2006), 193.
15. McCullough, *1776*, 191.
16. David Hackett Fischer, *Washington's Crossing* (Oxford University Press, 2006), 111.

17. McCullough, *1776*, 243.
18. Fischer, *Washington's Crossing*, 114.
19. McCullough, *1776*, 243.
20. McCullough, *1776*, 246.
21. McCullough, *1776*, 249, 257.
22. McCullough, *1776*, 269.
23. Letter from George Washington to John Augustine Washington, December 18, 1776, Founders Online, National Archives, https://www.firstinpeace.net/documents/letter-to-john-augustine-washington-december-18-1776/.
24. Ketanji Brown Jackson, *Lovely One: A Memoir* (Random House, 2024), 104.
25. Jackson, *Lovely One*, 109.
26. Jackson, *Lovely One*, 110.
27. Andrew C. McCarthy, "Senator Hawley's Disingenuous Attack Against Judge Jackson's Record on Child Pornography," *National Review*, March 20, 2022, https://www.nationalreview.com/2022/03/senator-hawleys-disingenuous-attack-against-judge-jacksons-record-on-child-pornography/.
28. Jackson, *Lovely One*, 375.
29. @Reverendwarnock, X, April 7, 2022, https://x.com/ReverendWarnock/status/1512172174974533634.
30. "Military Park: A Cultural Town Square," Newark City Parks, accessed October 19, 2025, https://newarkcityparks.org/military-park/.
31. Travis Shaw, "'Summer Soldiers and Sunshine Patriots'—The American Crisis," American Battlefield Trust, accessed October 19, 2025, https://www.battlefields.org/learn/articles/summer-soldiers-and-sunshine-patriots-american-crisis.
32. Fischer, *Washington's Crossing*, 140.
33. Shaw, "'Summer Soldiers and Sunshine Patriots.'"
34. Fischer, *Washington's Crossing*, 142.
35. Shaw, "'Summer Soldiers and Sunshine Patriots.'"

9. Grace

1. Helen O'Neill, "In Twilight of Life, a Racist Mourns His Violent Past," *The Salt Lake Tribune*, April 2, 2009, https://archive.sltrib.com/story.php?ref=/ci_12055420.
2. Tracy Smith, "Federal Judge Whose Son Was Killed in Ambush: 'My Son's Death Cannot Be in Vain,'" *CBS News*, September 11, 2021, https://www.cbsnews.com/news/esther-salas-son-murder-roy-den-hollander-48-hours/.
3. Tom Casey, Drew Dickson, and Dennis Dolan, hosts, *Deacons Pod*, podcast, "Judge Esther Salas," August 2, 2022, https://paulist.org/the-conversation/deacons-pod-judge-esther-salas/.
4. Danny's Pantry homepage, accessed October 19, 2025, https://dannyspantry.org/#about-us.
5. Casey, Dickson, and Dolan, "Judge Esther Salas."
6. Hannah Robbins, "Why Is Politically Motivated Violence on the Rise in the U.S.?" *The Hub*, June 23, 2025.

10. Vision

1. James Reaney, *Lewis Carroll's Alice Through the Looking Glass* (Porcupine's Quill, 1995), 69.
2. James Baldwin, *The Fire Next Time* (Dial Press, 1963), 140.
3. Raj Chetty et al., "The Fading American Dream: Trends in Absolute Income Mobility Since 1940," National Bureau of Economic Research, Working Paper 22910, December 2016.
4. Juliana Menasce Horowitz, Ruth Igielnik, and Rakesh Kochhar, "Most Americans Say There Is Too Much Income Inequality in the U.S., but Fewer Than Half Call It a Top Priority, 1. Trends in Income and Wealth Inequality," Pew Research Center, January 9, 2020, https://www.pewresearch.org/social-trends/2020/01/09/most-americans-say-there-is-too-much-economic-inequality-in-the-u-s-but-fewer-than-half-call-it-a-top-priority/.
5. Sabrina Malhi, "Childbirth Deadlier for Americans, Especially Black Women, Study Finds," *Washington Post,* June 4, 2024,

https://www.washingtonpost.com/health/2024/06/04/us-maternal-mortality-rate-higher-other-countries/.

6. John August, "Healthcare Insights: How Medical Debt Is Crushing 100 Million Americans," ILR Scheinman Institute, October 21, 2024, https://www.ilr.cornell.edu/scheinman-institute/blog/john-august-healthcare/healthcare-insights-how-medical-debt-crushing-100-million-americans.
7. Martin Luther King Jr., Nobel Peace Prize acceptance speech, December 10, 1964, https://www.nobelprize.org/prizes/peace/1964/king/acceptance-speech/.
8. Ross A. Thompson, "Early Brain Development and Public Health," *Delaware Journal of Public Health*, October 18, 2024, https://pubmed.ncbi.nlm.nih.gov/39493243/.

INDEX

About the Author

Kevin Lowery

Cory Booker is the senior United States senator from New Jersey. Booker earned bachelor's and master's degrees at Stanford University, attended Oxford University as a Rhodes Scholar, and earned a law degree at Yale University. He served as mayor of Newark before becoming New Jersey's first Black senator and only the fourth popularly elected Black senator in US history. Booker is a national leader in the effort to expand economic opportunity and create safe, strong, nurturing communities for every American family. He lives in Newark's Central Ward.